Is Geography Destiny?

Is Geography Destiny?

LESSONS FROM LATIN AMERICA

John Luke Gallup
Alejandro Gaviria
Eduardo Lora

INTER-AMERICAN DEVELOPMENT BANK

A COPUBLICATION OF STANFORD SOCIAL SCIENCES, AN IMPRINT OF
STANFORD UNIVERSITY PRESS, AND THE WORLD BANK

©2003   Inter-American Development Bank
         1300 New York Avenue, N.W.
         Washington, D.C. 20577

1 2 3 4 06 05 04 03

A copublication of Stanford Social Sciences, an imprint of Stanford
University Press, and the World Bank.

Stanford University Press   The World Bank
1450 Page Mill Road   1818 H Street, N.W.
Palo Alto, Calif. 94304   Washington, D.C. 20433

The views and opinions expressed in this publication are those of the
authors and do not necessarily reflect the official position of the Inter-
American Development Bank.

ISBN 0-8213-5451-5 (World Rights except North America)
ISBN 0-8047-4927-2 (North America)

Library of Congress Cataloging-in-Publication Data

Gallup, John Luke, 1962-
    Is geography destiny? / John Luke Gallup, Alejandro Gaviria, and
      Eduardo Lora. p. cm.
    "Latin American Development Forum."
    Includes bibliographical references and index.
    ISBN 0-8213-5451-5
      1. Latin America—Economic conditions. 2. Economic geography.
    I. Gaviria, Alejandro, 1966- II. Lora, Eduardo, 1953- III. Title.

    HC125.G255 2003
    330.98—dc21

                                                    2003043288

Latin American Development Forum Series

This series was created in 2003 to promote debate, disseminate information and analysis, and convey the excitement and complexity of the most topical issues in economic and social development in Latin America and the Caribbean. It is sponsored by the Inter-American Development Bank, the United Nations Economic Commission for Latin America and the Caribbean, and the World Bank. The manuscripts chosen for publication represent the highest quality in each institution's research and activity output, and have been selected for their relevance to the academic community, policymakers, researchers, and interested readers.

Advisory Committee Members

Inés Bustillo, Director, Washington Office, Economic Commission for Latin America and the Caribbean, United Nations

Guillermo Calvo, Chief Economist, Inter-American Development Bank

Jose Luis Guasch, Regional Adviser, Latin America and Caribbean Region, World Bank

Stephen Haber, A. A. and Jeanne Welch Milligan Professor, Department of Political Science, Stanford University; Peter and Helen Bing Senior Fellow, the Hoover Institution

Eduardo Lora, Principal Adviser, Research Department, Inter-American Development Bank

José Antonio Ocampo, Executive Secretary, Economic Commission for Latin America and the Caribbean, United Nations

Guillermo E. Perry, Chief Economist, Latin America and Caribbean Region, World Bank

Luis Servén, Lead Economist, Latin America and Caribbean Region, World Bank

About the Authors

John Luke Gallup is an independent economic researcher studying problems of poverty, geography, and health in developing countries. His current project uses earthworms to clean up Agent Orange in Vietnam. He recently taught economics and was a research fellow at the Center for International Development at Harvard University. He received a Ph.D. in economics and an M.A. in demography from the University of California, Berkeley.

Alejandro Gaviria is the deputy director of the Planning Department in Colombia. He has been deputy of Fedesarrollo, Colombia's leading policy research institution, and researcher of the Inter-American Development Bank. He has written widely on social and institutional topics. His most recent publications include journal articles on crime and victimization, social mobility, and corruption, as well as a book on educational policy in Colombia. He holds a Ph.D. from the University of California, San Diego.

Eduardo Lora is the principal adviser of the Research Department of the Inter-American Development Bank and has served as coordinator of the Bank's annual report *Economic and Social Progress in Latin America.* He has been an associate member of Saint Antony's College of Oxford University, editor of *Coyuntura Economica,* and executive director of Fedesarrollo. His numerous publications include an economic statistics textbook and an introductory textbook on the Colombian economy. He holds an M.Sc. in economics from the London School of Economics.

Contents

MAPS

TABLES

Preface

SOMETIMES THE MOST CANDID QUESTIONS are the most interesting. Why are some countries poorer than others? Why do some countries in Latin America fail to grow at a satisfactory pace even when they have followed all the suggestions prescribed by economists? Why are inequalities greater in Latin American societies than in other developing regions?

Although the Research Department of the Inter-American Development Bank (IDB) is made up of economists, we recognized that answering such questions involves entering into terrain beyond economics. By 1998, we were already studying the influence of demographic factors and had launched some studies on the effects of political institutions on the quality of Latin American governments. But data and intuition were telling us that something was still missing. Inspired by the works of such noted authors as those cited in the introduction to this book, we began a series of studies on the influence of geography on Latin American development. Since the capabilities of the Research Department in this area were limited, those in charge of the project (Eduardo Lora and Alejandro Gaviria) decided to link up with John Luke Gallup, then a researcher at the Center for International Development at Harvard University. He was already working on the issue of geography with Jeffrey Sachs. We also decided to contract some exploratory studies in several countries under the auspices of the IDB's Latin American Research Network. The IDB created this network in 1991 to strengthen policy formulation and contribute to the development policy agenda in Latin America. Through a competitive bidding process, the network provided grant funding for nine case studies based on an open research agenda, so that each team could best utilize the information available in the country and explore different angles of research. It was a risky strategy, but one that ultimately proved fruitful not only for our study but also for the centers involved. Several of them have found new areas of research related to geography, such as road infrastructure, health, and political and fiscal decentralization.

The authors of the original Latin American Research Network studies were María Carmen Choque, Erwin Galoppo, Luis Carlos Jemio, Rolando Morales, and Natacha Morales (CIESS-ECONOMETRICA SRL, Bolivia); Lykke Andersen, Eduardo Antelo, José Luis Evia, Osvaldo Nina, and Miguel Urquiola (Universidad Católica Boliviana, Bolivia); Carlos R. Azzoni, Narcio Menezes-Filho, Tatiane A. de Menezes, and Raul Silveira-Neto (FIPE-Fundação Instituto de Pesquisas Econômicas, Brazil); Denisard Alves, Robert Evenson, Elca Rosenberg, and Christopher Timmins (University of São Paulo, Brazil); Ricardo Bitrán, Cecilia Má, and Gloria Ubilla (Bitrán y Asociados, Chile); Jairo Núñez Méndez and Fabio Sánchez Torres (CEDE, Universidad de los Andes, Colombia); Gerardo Esquivel (Centro de Estudios Económicos, Colegio de México, México); Roberto Blum and Alberto Díaz Cayeros (CIDAC, Centro de Investigación para el Desarrollo, Mexico); and Javier Escobal and Máximo Torero (GRADE, Grupo de Análisis para el Desarrollo, Peru).

This book has also benefited from the generous collaboration of several people. Special mention must be made of Céline Charvériat, who alerted us to the devastating effects of natural disasters in Latin America and prepared the section on that issue in chapter 1, as well as several sections on the possibilities for urban and regional policies that are incorporated into chapter 3. Mauricio Olivera and Jorge Cepeda had the time-consuming task of helping to prepare graphs and tables and compiling the files for publication. Several colleagues from the Research Department and other IDB departments made valuable suggestions and corrections, starting with Ricardo Hausmann, then Chief Economist at the IDB, who consistently lent his support to this project. Rita Funaro helped us reshape our early drafts and made useful editorial suggestions throughout.

Introduction

Is Geography Destiny?

ECONOMISTS AND OTHER SOCIAL SCIENTISTS have rediscovered geography after several decades of indifference and suspicion. The champions of this rediscovery have been intellectual figures of the stature of David Landes, Jared Diamond, and Jeffrey Sachs, to name only a few.

> [Geography] tells an unpleasant truth, namely, that nature like life is unpleasant, unequal in its favors; further, that nature's unfairness is not easily remedied . . . . Yet, it would be a mistake to see geography as destiny. Its significance can be reduced or evaded, though invariably at a price. . . . Defining away or ignoring the problem will not make it go away or help us solve it.
>
> *David Landes*

> The striking difference between the long-term histories of peoples of the different continents has been due not to innate differences in the peoples themselves but to differences in their environments.
>
> *Jared Diamond*

> If social scientists were to spend more time looking at maps, they would be reminded of the powerful geographical patterns in economic development.
>
> *Jeffrey Sachs*

This renaissance represents the triumph of reason and science over suspicion and supposition. It dismisses the epithets—"determinist," "reductionist," "fatalist," and "racist"—hurled at those who claim that geographical conditions influence development. After all, the evidence is there. Location, climate, and terrain do make a difference. Are they the only factors that matter for development? Of course not. Is geography destiny? Perhaps, if its importance is ignored.

Disillusionment with geography led many universities to close their geography departments after World War II. One of the few that retained these studies was the London School of Economics. Its motto reads *Rerum cognoscere causas*—knowing the cause is ultimately the aim of all scientific research. All science is based on the relation between cause and effect. Anything that is not determined by a cause is random and therefore beyond any effort at discernment. In that respect, "determinism" is a sounder position than skepticism, which entails surrendering to ignorance. But no serious researcher believes that any single factor, no matter how important, can by itself determine social outcomes such as slavery, poverty, or development. It is always from the interplay between some conditions and others that outcomes may—only may—arise. Not surprisingly, social researchers, especially economists, have made probabilistic theory and its empirical applications part and parcel of their tool kit.

Scientists use experiments to isolate the influence of the many factors that may influence a phenomenon. The speed of a falling body depends not only on the force of gravity, but also on the resistance of that body to the air, which is in turn determined by its shape and other physical characteristics. To prove that the law of gravity is a "law," these factors have to be isolated, for example, by using a vacuum chamber.

In the social sciences, there are no such pure experiments, but social scientists do have ways to create their own vacuum chambers where they can observe the influence of a single factor on a phenomenon of interest. Economists, for example, use econometrics to study how change in one variable (the explanatory variable) affects the phenomenon of interest (the dependent variable) when other relevant variables are held constant. For methodological reasons, science is therefore "reductionist." There is nothing wrong with this approach, provided one does not lose sight of the context. Once it is established that the force of gravity influences all bodies alike, regardless of their weight, shape, or size, it must again be remembered that not all bodies fall at the same speed. For our purposes, proving the influence of geography on development does not mean denying other factors.

"Geography" is a concept encompassing various dimensions, which is tantamount to saying that geography affects development through not just one but many channels. This book distinguishes between physical channels, such as the productivity of land, rainfall, or temperature, and human channels, such as the location of populations with respect to coasts or urban centers. The process of isolating each of these influences is complex. As in any other scientific effort, the correct answer is not always attained on the first try.

In Latin America, both geographical conditions and the results of the development process vary widely. There are regions where income levels and health conditions do not differ substantially from those typical of Africa. But there are also cities where income, health, and education are much closer to patterns in the industrial world than to what is typical of the developing world. Has geography had something to do with these results? More important, can the influence of geography be directed toward developing the disadvantaged countries and regions?

Determinism and Fatalism

To take up these questions, this book accepts the degree and type of determinism that is characteristic of any scientific research, but rejects any suggestion of fatalism. It is a mistake to equate determinism with fatalism. As an example, genetic predisposition to a stroke is a fact that cannot be changed, but knowing about it may mean the difference between a premature death and a long life (even if a stroke is the ultimate cause of death). Of course, the difference lies not in the knowledge itself but in whether the predisposed person decides to follow through on medical recommendations for his or her health. Hence, determinism does not imply anything about what can or cannot be done. Determinism does not inhibit our freedom, but actually expands it by arming us with knowledge that we can use to change the way our own conditions affect us. Ridley (1999), author of various books popularizing science, writes: "Freedom lies in expressing your own determinism, not somebody else's. It is not the determinism that makes a difference, but the ownership" (p. 313).

In the world of the social sciences, geography tends to be accorded a treatment similar to that given to genetics in the world of medical and biological sciences some time ago. If genetics cannot be changed, of what use could it be, and if it can be changed, what sense could there be to altering nature's wise designs? Fatalism with regard to genetics had nothing to do with genetics itself, but with the prejudices of its potential users and beneficiaries. Popular opposition to genetics has not completely disappeared, but knowledge of genetics has now moved to a point beyond that discussion. Molecular biology is going to profoundly change the medical disciplines, and eventually our lives as well. That will be true even should scientists completely refrain from any kind of genetic manipulation or selection. The arsenal of information provided by genes is useful for detecting propensity for diseases, understanding what causes them and how they unfold, and, ultimately, for preventing, treating, and curing them.

It would be an exaggeration to say that geography is to the development of societies what genetics is to the development of living beings (although both processes are closely connected, as Jared Diamond [1997] has shown). But the parallel is useful for emphasizing that it is incorrect to equate determinism with fatalism, even though some factors determining who we are (as human beings or as societies) cannot be changed. Indeed, some geographical factors are a constraint to development, but understanding them and designing appropriate policies to deal with them can help countries liberate themselves from these constraints.

The parallel between geography and genetics is also useful because both disciplines have been tainted by racist interpretations resulting from the prejudices of some of their earlier proponents. In the 1920s, Ellsworth Huntington, one of the first to methodically study the relationship between geography and culture, popularized the thesis that physical environment and racial inheritance are the two determinants of character and willingness to work, and hence of the progress of societies (Huntington 1927). For decades, Francis Galton and his Eugenics Society argued that "the races can be improved" through a deliberate selection process (Galton 1889, cited by Weiner 1999, p. 92). This notion gained a great deal of acceptance in academic and government circles in the United States and several European countries. But, tragically, the process finally played itself out with the racial experiments and sterilization campaigns of the Nazis as part of the Holocaust. Then came shame and expiation, which resulted in the rejection of the disciplines associated with those horrors.

A half century later, studies of genetics have come to show overwhelmingly that there is no biological basis for the concept of race. The reading of the human genome has shown that there are no systematic differences in genes among the different races, and that the concept of race is cultural and sociological rather than biological. Thus, advancing knowledge in a discipline not long ago repudiated as racist will be responsible for freeing us from racist prejudices.

Something similar is taking place with the study of geography. The central thesis in the work of Jared Diamond is that differences in natural conditions, not differences between some peoples and others, explain variations in development patterns. Looking for the keys to development in geography—the study of the earth, its characteristics, and the life it supports—challenges charges of racism with its very definition.

Three Viewpoints

The channels through which geography influences economic and social development can be studied at different levels and perspectives of time. In chapter 1 countries are the basic unit of observation, and some historical considerations notwithstanding, the horizon of analysis is limited to the past four or five decades. The objective is to establish to what extent geography is responsible for differences in development between countries, and more specifically between Latin America and other groups of countries. The economic and social development of Latin American countries has been and continues to be affected both by physical geography (climate and the characteristics of land and topography) and by human geography (settlement patterns of the population). The most significant channels of influence of geography are the productivity of the land, the presence of endemic diseases, natural disasters, the location of countries and their populations in relation to the coast, and the concentration of the population in urban areas.

In chapter 2, the level of observation is that of regions within Latin American countries with the greatest geographical diversity: Bolivia, Brazil, Colombia, Mexico, and Peru. Using different historical perspectives depending on the country, this chapter analyzes the influence of geography on regional economic inequalities, patterns of spatial concentration of the population, and regional variations in patterns of health. Although the country studies limit the field of observation, they offer some advantages over the comparative international approach. First, they make it possible to isolate the influence of national factors that cannot be controlled in international comparisons, such as institutions or culture. Inasmuch as these factors vary less within each country than between countries, it is more feasible in national studies to capture the influence of geography in a purer form. Second, an analysis by country makes it possible to better separate channels of influence, since more detailed and homogeneous information can be used. It also makes it possible to combine statistical information with historical and ethnographic evidence, which would be difficult to incorporate into comparisons between many countries. The results of this chapter ratify many of the results in chapter 1, but they also draw attention to the presence of complex interactions between geography, institutions, and weather patterns.

The first two chapters look backward to determine whether geography is one of the causes explaining the current development levels of Latin American countries and the regions within them. In contrast, chapter 3 looks ahead at what can be done. The answer to some geographical disadvantages can be more and better roads and communications, although some solutions may be beyond what some countries can do, especially those that are poorer because their geography is more adverse. But the range of possible solutions does not stop there. Most policy instruments that can influence the effects of geography are not new: regional or urban development policies, research and technology programs, or decentralization strategies. What is new is that these policies can better incorporate the various geographical variables that influence their effectiveness. Failure to incorporate those variables into policies translates into welfare losses for the poorest people in the Latin American countries.

1

The Channels of Influence of Geography: Latin America from an International Perspective

IN THE FACE OF CONSIDERABLE EVIDENCE and suffering that points to its ongoing connections with development, geography remains largely ignored in discussions of public policy in Latin America. Hurricanes and earthquakes cause enormous damage, injuries, and death that are preventable; thousands of people suffer from endemic diseases for which cure or treatment continues to be elusive; rural families remain mired in poverty because of the poor productivity of their lands and the lack of appropriate technologies; and countless Latin Americans congregate in cities without access to basic infrastructure. Furthermore, in several regions in Latin America, there remains the problem of excluded indigenous communities and other racial minorities who, for historical reasons, are located in geographically disadvantaged areas. The physical, economic, and social isolation of these areas tends to reinforce the development gaps between these groups and the rest of society.

All of these problems and many others that will emerge throughout this book are the result of geography and its relationship to the societies of Latin America over the course of history. Many of the painful effects of these problems could have been prevented or mitigated had the influence of geography been better understood. Although many geographical conditions such as climate and location cannot be changed, their influence can be controlled or channeled toward the goals of economic and social development.

Geography affects development through the interaction between the physical characteristics of the landscape—such as climate, topography, and soil quality—and the settlement patterns of populations.

7

This chapter looks at how these interactions affect economic and social development from an international perspective—as opposed to the intranational perspective that will be adopted in chapter 2.

The objective is not to discuss the influences operating in the opposite direction—that is, from development (or its lack thereof) to geography. Thus, this chapter does not consider the effects of erosion, pollution, and overexploitation of natural resources on environmental sustainability, which, admittedly, may affect the very possibilities of development over the long run. Curiously, these channels of influence have been subjects of more analysis than has the more immediate effect of geography on development.

Geography influences economic and social development through four basic channels: productivity of lands, health conditions, the frequency and intensity of natural disasters, and access to markets. Naturally, these channels interact with the spatial distribution of the population and production, which are in turn largely endogenous to geographical factors. Urbanization, for example, increases the vulnerability of natural disasters and attenuates the effects of bad soils and vulnerability to vector-borne diseases.

These channels of influence can be modified through a variety of policies that will be discussed in chapter 3. Land productivity and health conditions can be changed through technological developments and the provision of certain basic services. The destructive potential of natural disasters can be offset through establishing adequate building standards and by locating housing in safer areas. Access to markets can be improved with investments in infrastructure. Urbanized areas can function more effectively if cities have adequate service infrastructure, incentive systems, and public administration. These and other policies can be identified and designed to turn geography into an advantage, but only if, as a first step, there is an understanding of the different channels through which physical and human geography influences the potential for economic and social development.

The Diverse Geographical Regions of Latin America

Latin America is largely located within tropical zones, but its geographical features span a variety of climates and ecozones, not all of them characteristic of tropical regions. One of the first climatic classification systems was that of Wladimir Köppen, developed a century ago but still the most useful and widely used today. Köppen's ecozones, shown in map 1.1 (p. 19), are based on temperature and precipitation data, as well as elevation (as modified by Geiger; see Strahler and Strahler 1992, pp. 155–60). The main ecozones in Latin America are tropical (A), dry (B), temperate (C), and high elevation (H). The ecozones allow us to identify the region's major geographical differences: temperate versus tropical, highlands versus tropical lowlands, and dry versus temperate outside of the tropics.

Several other geographical factors besides climate have had a strong impact on economic activity and population distribution in the region. Coastal areas are distinct from the inland; northern Mexico is unique because it borders the huge U.S. market; and direct access by sea to Europe historically has differentiated the Caribbean and Atlantic coast from the Pacific coast. The overlapping of the Köppen ecozones with these simple patterns of location forms the basis of the seven geographical zones for the region: border, tropical highlands, lowland Pacific coast, lowland Atlantic coast, Amazon, highland and dry Southern Cone, and the temperate Southern Cone (see map 1.2, p. 20).

Different Geographical Zones, Different Economic Outcomes

The border zone comprises the arid or temperate climate in the north of Mexico. This zone is sparsely populated, has higher average per capita gross domestic product (GDP) than the rest of Mexico and Latin America, and contains most of the Mexican *maquiladora* manufacturing assembly industry because of its proximity to the U.S. market (see maps 1.3 and 1.4, pp. 21 and 22, respectively).

The tropical highlands cover the highland regions of Central America and the Andean countries north of the Tropic of Capricorn. This zone has very high population densities despite its difficult access to the coast, and is home to most of the indigenous people of Latin America. Overall, it has the lowest per capita GDP on the continent, despite including Mexico City and Bogota, which have high-income levels relative to the rest of Latin America. The problems of this zone highlight what happens when populations continue to live in areas with geographical disadvantages. Poverty persists when the geographical barriers people face cannot be overcome, and when they do not move to more geographically favored regions.

The lowland Pacific and Atlantic coastal zones are tropical, with some small areas of dry ecozone. The Pacific coast has the highest population density of the seven geographical zones (with the notable exception of the sparsely populated Darien region along the Colombian and Panama border). The Atlantic coast also has dense population, though less so than the Pacific. The two coastal zones have per capita GDP about 20 percent higher than the highland zone they abut, with similarly high population concentrations. The coastal zones have better access to the sea and international trade, but must face the burden of disease and the agricultural challenges of a tropical environment.

The Amazon zone is still largely uninhabited in comparison with the other geographical zones, despite migration and the accompanying environmental consequences that have occurred over recent decades. Perhaps surprisingly, per capita GDP in the Amazon is higher than that in adjacent coastal and highland zones. This is mainly due to resource rents. Much of the GDP of the region comes from natural resource rents of mining and large plantations that are often owned by investors who do not reside in the jungle. Thus, GDP per capita is probably much higher than average household incomes per capita.

The two Southern Cone zones are both high-income areas. The temperate Southern Cone has a high population density, while the highland and dry Southern Cone has a population density barely higher than that of the Amazon. Average GDP per capita and the population density of the temperate Southern Cone are somewhat less than they would otherwise be because of the inclusion of temperate ecozones in Paraguay and Bolivia, both landlocked and poorer countries.

Looking at the average income levels and population densities of the geographical zones in table 1.1, the four tropical zones have the lowest GDP per capita, clustered around $5,000 (in 1995 dollars),

Table 1.1 Characteristics of Latin American Geographical Zones

Geographical zone	GDP per capita (1995$)	Population density (persons/ km²)	GDP density ($1,000/ km²)	Area (millions of km²)	Population within 100 km of coast (%)
Tropical highlands	4,343	52	226	1.9	11
Lowland Pacific coast	4,950	61	302	0.8	95
Lowland Atlantic coast	5,216	46	240	2.2	83
Amazon	5,246	6	31	9	1
Temperate Southern Cone	7,552	35	264	3.2	31
Mexican–U.S. border	7,861	17	134	1.1	30
Highland and dry Southern Cone	9,712	7	68	2.2	16

Source: Authors' calculations from data in maps 1.2, 1.3, and 1.4 (pp. 20–22).

except for the highlands at $4,343. The three temperate regions in the Southern Cone and northern Mexico have much higher income, averaging from $7,500 to $10,000. Population densities follow a very different pattern, with very low densities in the arid Southern Cone and Mexican border zones, intermediate in the temperate Southern Cone, and higher in the tropical coastal and highland zones.

The result of GDP per capita and population density is the density of economic production by land area. The zones with the highest economic production are the three densely populated tropical zones and the temperate Southern Cone. The Mexican border region is intermediate and the arid Southern Cone and the Amazon are very low. Although the GDP densities are similar across these groups of tropical and temperate zones, the temperate regions achieve higher GDP per capita with a lower population density, while the tropical regions struggle with the opposite combination.

The diversity of geographical conditions within Latin America is also apparent in some of its countries. While the Bahamas, El Salvador, Trinidad and Tobago, and Uruguay are homogeneous—that is, most of their territory belongs to only one main ecozone—countries like Bolivia, Brazil, Ecuador, Colombia, and Peru show an astonishing geographical diversity. Few other countries in the world offer so many climate zones and landscapes. Peru, for example, contains 84 of the 104 ecological regions in the world (according to one classification) and 28 different climates (see chapter 2). The geographical diversity of some Latin American countries has led to severe geographical fragmentation, as reflected in patterns of population settlement, at times with dire political consequences (see Inter-American Development Bank 2000, chapter 4). An index of geographical fragmentation of the population discussed in box 1.1 finds that Latin American countries have the greatest geographical fragmentation in the world.

Box 1.1 An Index of Geographical Fragmentation of the Population

In political science the fragmentation of a population is usually measured as the probability that two individuals taken at random from the population do not belong to the same group. We borrow this approach to define geographical fragmentation as the probability that two individuals taken at random do not live in similar ecozones. This measure goes from zero (which corresponds to a case where all the population is settled in the same ecozone) to one (which corresponds to the implausible case where each individual lives in a different ecozone). In general,

(Box continues on the following page.)

Box 1.1 (continued)

fragmentation will increase as the number of ecozones grows and the weight of each group equalizes.

Geographical fragmentation is a concept usually neglected by economists and even by political scientists. This is surprising because many social and economic cleavages have geographical underpinnings. Culture usually differs widely among inhabitants of different ecozones—for example, the contrast between outgoing and vocal lowlanders and timid and taciturn highlanders has become one of our most veritable cliches. Similarly, the composition of the economy differs widely among ecozones (for example, crops, minerals, and proximity to the ocean are in general different from one zone to another). Thus, geographical fragmentation is a dimension of social conflict and as such can play a pivotal role in politics in particular and in policymaking and development in general.

Figure 1.1 compares Latin America to other regions in terms of geographical fragmentation. Latin America is more fragmented than any

Figure 1.1 Index of Geographical Fragmentation

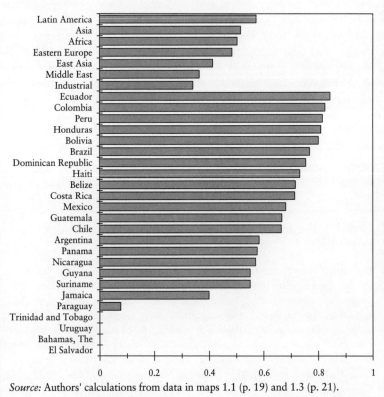

Source: Authors' calculations from data in maps 1.1 (p. 19) and 1.3 (p. 21).

other region of the world. The differences within Latin America are also substantial. The most geographically fragmented countries are Ecuador, Colombia, and Peru, and the least are the Bahamas, El Salvador, Trinidad and Tobago, and Uruguay.

Another type of fragmentation—ethnolinguistic fragmentation—has received much more attention from economists and political scientists alike. It is defined similarly as the probability that two persons taken at random speak different languages. While Latin America's geographical fragmentation is very high, figure 1.2 shows that its level of ethnolinguistic fragmentation is relatively low compared to other developing regions. In many countries there is a predominant language (Spanish or English) spoken by all but a small portion of the population. This is not the case for all the countries, however. Ethnolinguistic fragmentation is particularly substantial in Suriname, followed by Bolivia, Guatemala, and Peru.

Figure 1.2 Index of Ethnolinguistic Fragmentation

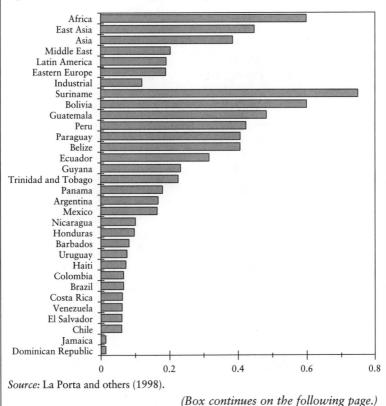

Source: La Porta and others (1998).

(Box continues on the following page.)

Box 1.1 (continued)

The conclusion that emerges is that the main lines of social division in Latin America are less ethnic than geographical. Geographical divisions imply that different groups of a society may face different conditions that affect their economic possibilities and may have different economic interests and social problems, all of which can influence the political game and, ultimately, all aspects of development.

History

The geographical remoteness and isolation of the Americas played a central role in the devastation of the indigenous people at the point of first contact with Europeans. Relative to the historical timeline, humans did not settle permanently in the Americas until quite recently, probably about 11,000 B.C. (see Diamond 1997, p. 49).[1] The first settlers were most likely small nomadic groups crossing the cold Bering Straits, so they carried few Old World diseases with them from northern Asia, in particular, no "crowd" diseases such as smallpox, measles, and typhus, and no tropical diseases. When Christopher Columbus arrived, followed by other conquistadors and explorers, the toll of Old World disease was catastrophic to the indigenous peoples of the New World, in some cases wiping out whole tribes before a shot was fired (many chilling examples are documented by Crosby 1972, 1986). The implausibly lopsided victories of Cortés over the Aztecs and Pizarro over the Incas are as much attributable to smallpox as to Spanish firearms and horses. The emperors of both the Incas and the Aztecs, along with large proportions of their populations, were killed by smallpox before the decisive battles with the Spaniards even began. By 1618, Mexico's initial population of about 20 million had collapsed to about 1.6 million (Diamond 1997, p. 210). According to McNeill (1976, p. 90), "ratios of 20:1 or even 25:1 between the pre-Columbian populations and the bottoming-out point in Amerindian population curves seem more or less correct, despite wide local variation."

Geography most likely played a hand in the pre-Columbian settlement patterns in the Americas. The main empires—the Aztec and the Inca—were in the tropical highlands, probably because of a better climate for agriculture and a more benign disease environment. With no use of seaborne trade, or even wheeled transport, access to the sea did not represent an economic advantage for these civilizations. The major exception to the highland New World civilizations was the Mayans in the tropical lowlands, but the dense population in the Yucatan peninsula mysteriously collapsed before contact with the Europeans.[2] The current concentration of indigenous peoples of Mexico, Central

America, and the Andean countries in the highlands is also a function of where indigenous people survived the introduction of Old World diseases. Highland populations were protected from the lowland tropical diseases of malaria, yellow fever, and hookworm, which contributed to the extinction of substantial Amerindian populations from most of the Caribbean islands.

Geography and Colonization

Colonization played a complicated but important role in shaping current patterns of economic development, but it is of little help in explaining the dramatic geographical variation in present-day Latin America. Most of the countries in the region share the same colonial heritage, despite very different economic outcomes. Among the countries with British, French, or Dutch rather than Iberian heritage, one can find some of the richest and also some of the poorest countries of the region.

Moreover, as shown by Diamond (1997), geography had a profound role in determining which countries were colonizers and which countries were colonized. Eurasia was highly favored relative to the other continents in terms of domesticable crops and livestock both by chance and because of its large area of contiguous ecological zones.[3] The constant proximity of settlements to their livestock and their own waste in Eurasia caused new diseases such as smallpox, measles, chickenpox, and a range of intestinal parasites. The concentration of sedentary populations in cities made possible by agricultural advances provided a constant pool of new vectors to sustain "crowd diseases" such as tuberculosis and influenza. This collection of infectious diseases proved to be devastating to unexposed populations and largely explains the easy conquest of the Americas and Australasia. The technological advances made possible by the agricultural advantages of Eurasia also explain the eventual European domination of Africa.

When Europeans brought Africans to the New World as slaves, they also imported a panoply of African diseases new to the Americas. Malaria, yellow fever, hookworm, schistosomiasis, and other diseases further devastated the indigenous population and have had a persistent impact on the disease burden since then. Most of these diseases remain major public health and economic problems in the American tropics to the present day.

The imported African diseases also plagued the European colonizers in the tropical regions of the New World, especially the Caribbean. Haiti was the graveyard for two large colonial armies (see box 1.2). Yellow fever and malaria devastated successive invasions by the British and the French, whose losses in Haiti were greater than the losses of either side at Waterloo (Heinl and Heinl 1978, p. 81).

Box 1.2 How the Climate of Haiti Destroyed Two Large
Armies

In the general chaos brought on by the French Revolution, the richest of
France's colonies, St. Domingue, later to become Haiti, began to slip
from her grasp. With the promulgation of the Rights of Man in a colony
based on a brutal system of slavery, armed resistance to the white
planters progressed from the mixed-race, pro-slavery *mulâtres* to a
general revolt by the African slaves by 1791.

Britain and Spain, both at war with Republican France in the 1790s,
agreed to divide the prize of St. Domingue between them. Spain fought
by proxy through the rebel slave bands in the north, but Britain invaded
with its own troops in the south in 1793. Realizing that neither Spain nor
Britain would brook an end to slavery, the rebels cast off the Spanish and
turned to attack the British. Though rarely directly engaged by the rebels
until near the end, the British succumbed to the geography of St.
Domingue. The British commander had assured London that he could
take the territory with 877 troops, but reinforcements could not keep up
with the ever-increasing toll of yellow fever and malaria. In a typical case,
Lieutenant Thomas Howard's regiment of 700 hussars lost 500 men in
one month with only seven battle deaths. In the end, disease and the
rebels forced the British to evacuate with more than 14,000 dead.
Edmund Burke summed up the debacle: "The hostile sword is merciful,
the country itself is the dreadful enemy."

When Napoleon consolidated his power in France after 1799, he
turned to reconquering the prized colony of St. Domingue to use it as a
springboard to reassert French control of the Louisiana Territory. His
downfall was the same as Britain's. French troops could not survive in
Haiti's disease-ridden environment. Leclerc, Napoleon's brother-in-law,
quickly occupied almost the whole colony with 20,000 troops in 1802.
Then yellow fever and malaria took hold. Mortality from yellow fever
exceeded 80 percent, and to hide the losses, the dead were carted away
at night and military funerals suspended. With all but two of his corps
commanders dead, Leclerc himself would succumb to yellow fever before
the year was out.

The French struggled on with massive reinforcements until 1803
before pulling out the surviving remnants of the army. Only 10,000 men
made it back to France, with 55,000 dead in the colony. The
hemisphere's second independent republic, Haiti, was born. It was to
provide refuge and support to Simón Bolívar in his darkest hour in 1815.
Napoleon was forced to give up his designs on the Louisiana Territory,
which he sold to the United States. The tenacity of the Haitian rebels was
essential to the only successful slave revolt in history, but victory
depended on Haiti's crushing burden of tropical disease.

Source: Heinl and Heinl (1978).

Slavery implied not only a new pool of diseases but profound changes in the composition of populations, the ability to exploit certain lands, and the patterns of institutional development of those countries that absorbed slaves in large numbers. Slavery was not a uniform phenomenon, but one clearly influenced by a combination of geographical, technological, and institutional factors (see box 1.3).

Box 1.3 Why Slavery Developed Only in Certain Regions

The relationship between geography and slavery has been the subject of extensive debate, motivated by the racist culture that evolved from colonists of European origin to justify the exploitation of blacks. The issue is to explain the concentration of slavery in tropical areas, since the large majority of slaves went to the Caribbean islands or Brazil, and in the United States they were concentrated in the subtropical south. The deep-seated justification given by the racist culture is that blacks were better able than whites to endure the unhealthy tropical environment.

Some of the most recent studies, which have their antecedents in the innovative findings of Thompson (1941), Williams (1964), and other authors, base their arguments on the conditions of production on plantations and the scarcity of other types of manual labor. Following this view, Engerman and Sokoloff (1997) have shown that slavery predominated in the tropics not because of its hostile disease environment, but because the institution of slavery was more economically productive on tropical plantations (though disastrous for those who actually did the work), while free labor was more productive in the temperate New World. The tropical climate was suitable for certain crops (sugar, tobacco, cacao, coffee, cotton, and rice) that were conducive to production on large-scale plantations, while temperate zones were conducive to grain-based agriculture with efficient smallholder production. Furthermore, the tropical plantation crops could be cultivated by gang labor forced to work rapidly without significant risk of damage to the crops. Hence, Engerman and Sokoloff argue that economies based on slave labor in Latin America and the Caribbean resulted in high levels of inequality with far-reaching consequences for institutions and economic development in these countries. The Spanish colonies had relatively little slavery, but the Amerindians, with a slave or serf-like status, made up a large percentage of the population in all these colonies until the end of the 19th century. This disparity resulted in high inequality and restrictive economic institutions similar to those in the slave states. According to Engerman and Sokoloff, the institutional environment (due to the historical but not persistent impact of geography) is what explains the divergence between Latin American economic performance and that of the United States and Canada.

(Box continues on the following page.)

Box 1.3 (continued)

Some authors, however, believe that health conditions in tropical areas could have been a factor in the predominance of black slavery over other races. Coelho and McGuire (1997) have argued that as a result of the exposure of many generations to tropical diseases, Africans had both greater genetic and acquired immunity to them, especially malaria, yellow fever, and hookworm. Most sub-Saharan African ethnic groups have two blood characteristics: the Duffy factor and the sickle cell trait. The Duffy factor confers immunity to the milder vivax form of malaria, while the sickle cell trait provides partial protection from the more deadly falciparum malaria. Most Africans were immune to yellow fever because of their exposure as children (when the disease is milder), and even nonimmune Africans have lower death rates from the disease for poorly understood reasons. Similarly, West Africans, from whom most New World slaves descended, have a clear but poorly understood tolerance to hookworm.

In any event, the ultimate explanation for the spatial concentration of black slavery is the scarcity of other types of manual labor in large-scale production units. Europeans engaged in or forced to work on plantations were allowed the opportunity to purchase lands and have the recourse to institutions whose protection did not extend to blacks. American Indian natives constituted a limited supply of manual labor that in many areas was decimated by diseases. A better resistance of blacks to certain tropical diseases possibly eased the process, although it neither explains nor justifies it.

In many regions of Latin America, present localization patterns of both black and indigenous populations still reflect elements from the past. Frequently, adverse climatic circumstances are reinforced by physical isolation and inadequate access to markets and infrastructure, as well as by various institutional and cultural mechanisms that make it difficult to obliterate the burden of history. Latin America still does not pay the attention to these problems that they deserve. Although this book does not address these issues in detail, it is motivated by the conviction that ignoring the impact of geography on development implies running the risk of ignoring ethnic minorities.

The Harsh but Not Indomitable Tropics

The difficulties of operating in a tropical environment were abundantly clear during the building of the Panama Canal. The effect of the humid tropics on everything from tools to clothing wrought havoc: "Anything made of iron or steel turned bright orange with rust. Books, shoes, belts, knapsacks, instrument cases, machete scabbards, grew mold overnight. Glued furniture fell apart. Clothes seldom ever dried" (McCullough 1977, p. 135).

Map 1.1 Köppen-Geiger Ecozones

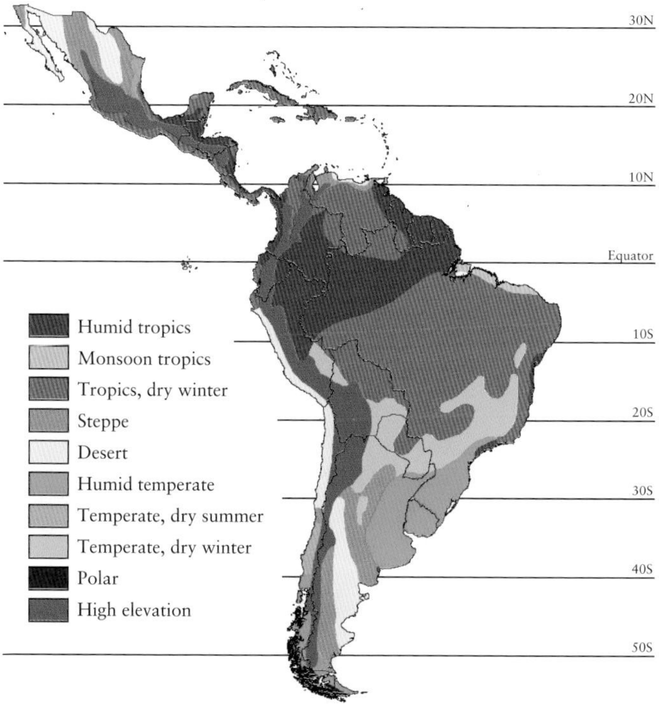

Source: Derived from Strahler and Strahler (1992).

Map 1.2 Geographical Zones

Source: Derived from Strahler and Strahler (1992).

Map 1.3 Population Density

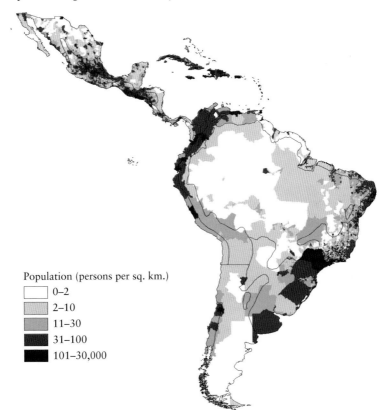

Population (persons per sq. km.)

- 0–2
- 2–10
- 11–30
- 31–100
- 101–30,000

Source: Calculations based on Tobler and others (1995).

Map 1.4 Regional GDP per Capita

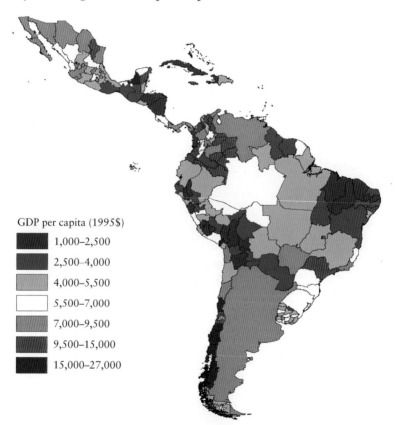

GDP per capita (1995$)

■	1,000–2,500
■	2,500–4,000
▨	4,000–5,500
□	5,500–7,000
▨	7,000–9,500
▨	9,500–15,000
■	15,000–27,000

Source: Azzoni and others (2000), Escobal and Torero (2000), Esquivel (1999), Morales and others (2000), Sánchez and Núñez (2000), Summers and Heston (1994), and Urquiola (1999).

Map 1.5 Distribution of per Capita Income

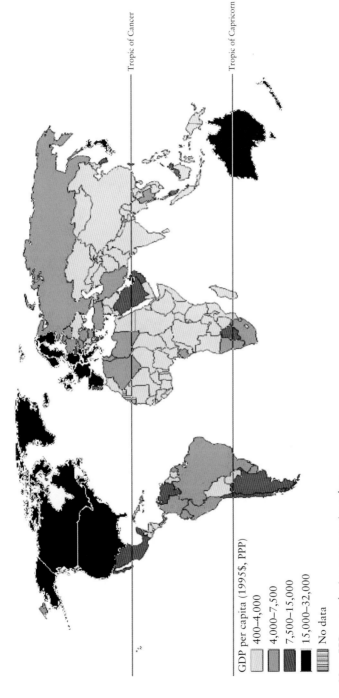

GDP per capita (1995$, PPP)

400–4,000
4,000–7,500
7,500–15,000
15,000–32,000
No data

Note: PPP = purchasing power parity values.
Source: Gallup, Sachs, and Mellinger (1999).

Map 1.6 Agricultural Output per Farmworker, 1994

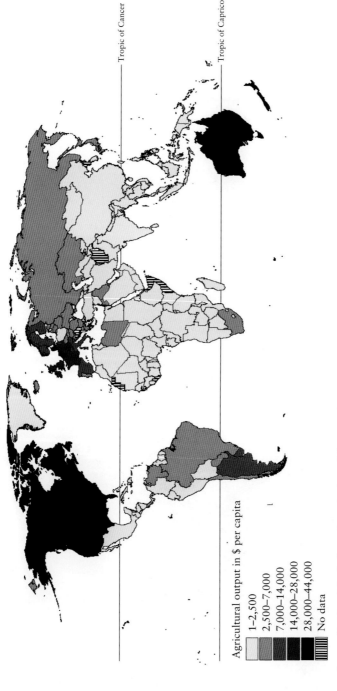

Agricultural output in $ per capita

1–2,500
2,500–7,000
7,000–14,000
14,000–28,000
28,000–44,000
No data

Source: Food and Agriculture Organization of the United Nations (1999).

Map 1.7 Extent of Malaria in Latin America, 1946–94

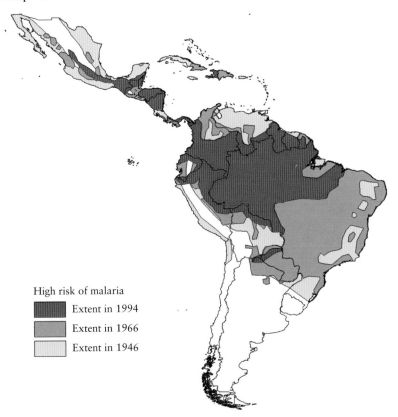

High risk of malaria
- Extent in 1994
- Extent in 1966
- Extent in 1946

Source: Pampana and Russell (1955) and World Health Organization (1967, 1997).

Map 1.8 Export Processing Zones in Latin America, 1997

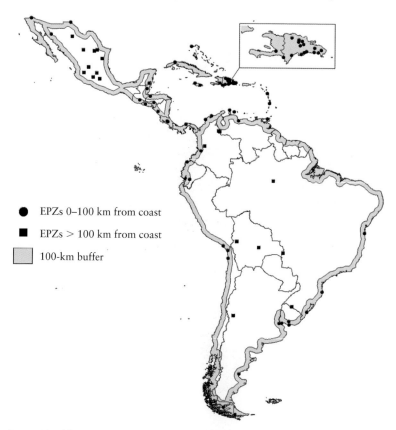

Source: World Economic Processing Zones Association (1997).

Above all, abandonment of the project by the French (1881–89) and the early failures by the Americans (1904–05) showed that intensive disease control, particularly for malaria and yellow fever, was a necessary condition for its completion.

Although the French made major investments in medical care, in the 1880s they did not yet understand the means of transmission of these two major mosquito-borne diseases. Besides the fearsome mortality of workers and the recurrent debilitation of those who survived, many of the most dynamic project leaders and engineers perished from tropical disease. On top of unrealistic technical goals and organizational difficulties, the loss from disease was more than the project could sustain. At least 20,000 lives were lost to disease during the nine years of the French effort (McCullough 1977, p. 235).

U.S. President Theodore Roosevelt, the prime mover behind the American attempt to build the canal, immediately recognized the importance of disease control from his own experiences in the tropics: "I feel that the sanitary and hygienic problems . . . on the Isthmus are those which are literally of the first importance, coming even before the engineering" (McCullough 1977, p. 406). When the Americans revived construction of the canal in 1904, a crucial element of their success was Dr. William Gorgas. He had demonstrated in Havana in 1901 what few believed possible: endemic yellow fever could be eliminated by intensive mosquito control. Once Gorgas was given substantial resources and support in 1905, he carried out a similar feat in Panama. In one of the most intensive vector control efforts before or since, Gorgas largely eliminated the threat of both yellow fever and malaria by denying mosquitoes the pools of stagnant water they need to breed. An army of health inspectors was used to go house to house. The provision of clean water and other public health measures reduced the incidence of other diseases as well. Contrary to popular impression, malaria was a greater threat to health than yellow fever in Panama, as Gorgas recognized, with higher mortality under both the French and American canal projects (McCullough 1977, p. 139).

Yellow fever is no longer a major public health problem because of a successful worldwide control effort in the 1930s and the development of an effective vaccine. The story of malaria is completely different. The worldwide eradication effort that started in the 1920s and intensified in the 1950s and 1960s was largely a failure in the tropics, and no vaccine strategies have yet proven viable. Currently, all the inexpensive drugs for treatment of and protection from malaria are losing their effectiveness in the face of resistant strains.

Geography and Development

Stark evidence of the strong and pervasive effects of geography on development is the fact that most of the world's poorer countries are located in the tropics, while the highest levels of development are found in nontropical areas (see map 1.5, p. 23).

If geography were unimportant, one would expect to see similar economic conditions throughout the world, subject to some random variation. In fact, poor countries are rarely interspersed in the richer regions, although a few rich countries can be found in the tropical areas.

Latin America has more middle-income countries in the tropics than do other regions with tropical areas, suggesting that it is less bound by the general rule that the tropics are poorer. The geographical gradients within Latin America are nevertheless clear and dramatic. Figure 1.3 shows that 1995 per capita GDP levels in the region follow roughly a U-shape in latitude, with much higher levels in the temperate south, and a minimum level just below the equator in the band from 20° south to 0° latitude. The geographical tropics is defined as the region from 23.45° south to 23.45° north, where the sun is directly overhead at some point

Figure 1.3 Mean GDP per Capita by Latitude Band in Latin America

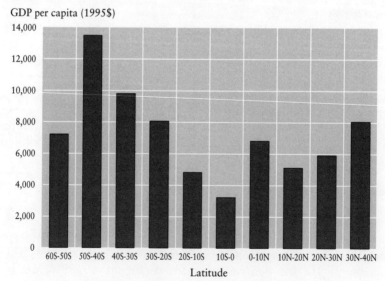

Note: GDP = gross domestic product, S = south, and N = north.
Sources: World Bank (1998) and Environmental Systems Research Institute (1996).

Figure 1.4 Income by Latitude in 1900
(current US$)

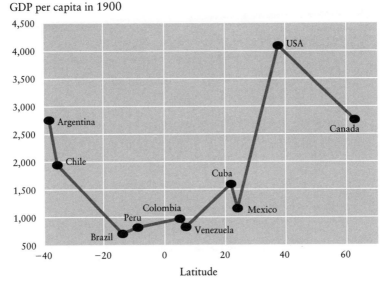

Source: GDP per capita data for 1900 are from Maddison (1995, table C-16d), except for Cuba in 1913, which is from Coatsworth (1998, table 1.1).

during the year. Tropical Latin America has much lower income levels than temperate South America or temperate Mexico, although some spots of high development can be found in the Caribbean. The average per capita GDP of $4,580 found in the 20° south to 0° latitude band is just under half the level found at high points in temperate regions.

The problem of poverty in the tropics is nothing new. The U-shaped gradient shown in figure 1.3 has persisted for as long as we have data. Figure 1.4 shows that per capita GDP in 1900 in the tropical countries of Brazil, Peru, Colombia, and Venezuela was less than half that of temperate Chile and Argentina, and lower than Mexico and Cuba on the tropical fringe. By a factor of three, the tropical Latin American countries had lower incomes than the United States or Canada, with their temperate climates.

Data for 1800 are more tenuous and sparse, but show the same pattern by latitude (see figure 1.5). The tropics were poorer than the temperate countries, with the clear exception of Cuba and, apparently, Haiti, whose richness was based on the brutally productive (but eventually unsustainable) slave economy.[4]

Since the Latin American countries share much of the same colonial and cultural history, current and past patterns of income by latitude

Figure 1.5 Income by Latitude in 1800
(current US$)

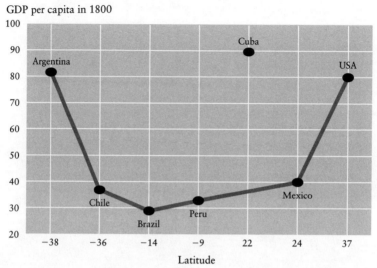

Source: Coatsworth (1998).

within the region are striking. While differences in economic development across continents are more likely due to divergent historical
experiences rather than to geography, this position is less plausible
within continents. The pattern of development within Latin America is
consistent with the pattern within Africa and Eurasia. The nontropical
northern and southern extremes of Africa are the wealthiest regions of
the continent. In East Asia, the tropical and subtropical regions are
poorer, in general, than the temperate north.

Population density is a rough indicator of how hospitable the land
is to an agrarian society, but there is no evidence of overpopulation as
an explanation for why the tropics are poorer. In fact, tropical areas
have fewer people on the land as well as lower per capita income levels.

Current population distribution in Latin America largely conforms
to the original European settlement patterns (including the slaves they
brought), plus indigenous highland populations that survived the
Columbian exchange. As with other regions of the world, population
shows a bimodal pattern with respect to latitude (see figure 1.6), with
peaks in the temperate middle latitudes and lower densities in the far
south and the tropics. The highest population densities in the tropical
10° to 20° north latitude band of central Mexico and Central America
are somewhat of an exception, but consistent with a relationship

Figure 1.6 Population Density by Latitude Band

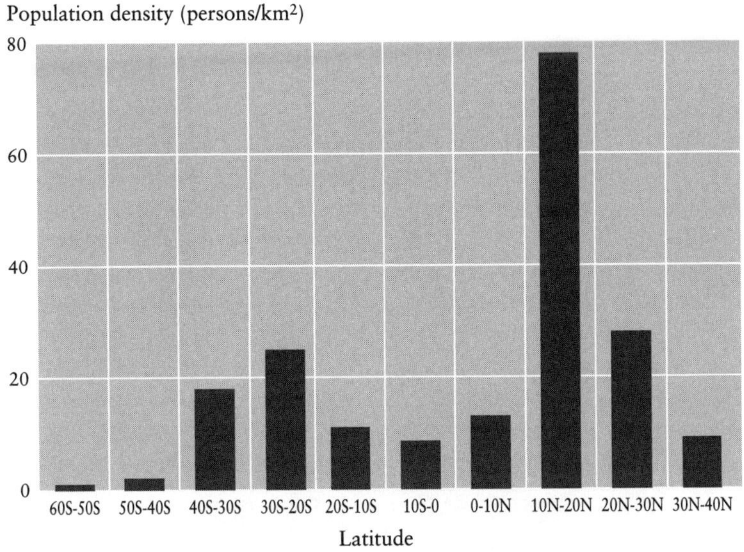

Population density (persons/km^2)

Latitude

Sources: World Bank (1997) and Environmental Systems Research Institute (1996).

between climate and population, since most of this population lives in the highlands with a temperate climate.

The low population density of the tropics in Latin America implies that the economic productivity of tropical land is even more unequally distributed than incomes in the region. Figure 1.7 shows that the economic output of land area in the tropical band of 10° south to 0° latitude is $39,000 per square kilometer (or about $97,500 per square mile), less than a quarter of the output at 20° to 30° north and south.

Tropical Agriculture

With factors such as history and population unable to explain the geographical variation, the evidence of economic disadvantage of tropical areas points to problems with agricultural productivity. Agricultural yields are particularly sensitive to climate, soil resources, and technology.

Climate and soil conditions are different in temperate and tropical ecological zones. Furthermore, the tremendous differences in the natural plant and animal communities of the tropics and the temperate zones suggest that the productivity of the narrow range of plants used

Figure 1.7 GDP Density by Latitude Band

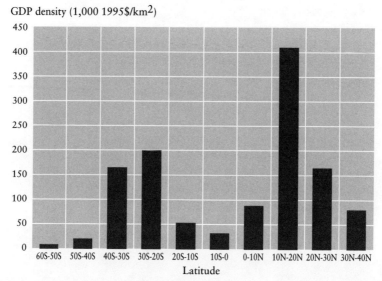

GDP density (1,000 1995$/km²)

Source: World Bank (1998) and Environmental Systems Research Institute (1996).

for agricultural staples would also be systematically different between the two regions. Although it is theoretically possible for food staples to be adapted to be equally productive in temperate and tropical zones, in practice this has not happened. Even after accounting for differences in input use in agriculture, tropical yields of principal crops are starkly lower than temperate yields.

This is only partly a natural phenomenon. Its main cause may be found in the pattern of technological developments originally spurred by the distribution of agriculture and animal species and land conditions, and reinforced by centuries of technological changes biased toward the richer areas. Technological progress is faster where markets are larger, finance is cheaper, and the protection of intellectual property rights assures that innovators can reap the benefit of their investments in developing new technologies. These factors, which tend to accentuate the technological gaps between rich and poor countries in general, are extremely important in the case of agricultural research and development nowadays, which has become a high-tech, large-scale activity performed by highly specialized firms.

The disparity between tropical and nontropical agricultural output per farmworker (see map 1.6, p. 24) is even more pronounced than the disparity between tropical and nontropical income levels (see map

1.5). Most individual crops tell the same story. Table 1.2 shows that nontropical yields are higher than tropical yields for 9 of 10 important crop categories. This is especially true for temperate crops like wheat, but also for some tropical crops like maize or sugar cane.

These differences could be due in part to the inputs used. Fertilizers, tractors, improved seeds, and labor all affect yields, regardless of whether the climate is ideal for the crop. Farmers in wealthier countries use more nonlabor inputs per hectare, which suggests that low yields in the tropics may be caused *by* poverty rather than be a cause *of* poverty. However, estimates by Gallup and Sachs (1999) show that tropical yields are much lower, even controlling for differences in input use.[5] Tropical and dry ecozones, which make up most of the geographical tropics, have yields 30 to 40 percent lower than temperate ecozones for the same input use. Moreover, agricultural productivity grew about 2 percent per year more slowly in tropical and dry ecozones than in temperate ones. Therefore, although the origin of the dif-

Table 1.2 Crop Yields in Tropical versus Nontropical Countries of the World, 1998

Crop	Tropical yield (mt/ha)[a]	Nontropical yield (mt/ha)[a]	Tropical/ nontropical	Statistically significant difference[b]
Cereals (milled rice equivalent)	16.5	26.9	0.61	x
Maize	20.1	45.1	0.45	x
Root crops (potato, cassava, etc.)	105.0	200.0	0.53	x
Sugar cane[c]	647.0	681.0	0.95	
Pulses (beans and peas)	7.9	13.3	0.59	x
Oilcrops	5.1	4.0	1.28	x
Vegetables	113.0	177.0	0.64	x
Fruits	96.0	97.9	0.98	
Bananas	155.0	201.0	0.77	x
Coffee	6.5	15.4	0.42	x
Observations[d]	108.0	95.0		

a. Metric tons per hectare.

b. x = p value less than 5 percent for t test that mean tropical yield is different from mean nontropical yield.

c. Data are for 1996.

d. This is the number of observations for cereals. Not all countries produce root crops.

Source: Food and Agriculture Organization of the United Nations (1999).

ferences in productivity may be natural, there is no doubt that technological developments over time have widened the gap. Technological
advances have been concentrated in the wealthier regions, whose more
homogeneous ecology facilitates the diffusion of successful species and
technologies.[6]

While some crops such as tree nuts or tropical fruits are clearly
more productive in the tropics, few of them are major parts of the food
system. Table 1.3 shows the contribution of different crop categories
to the world food supply. Cereals provide half of all calories and
almost as much of protein consumption. Oilcrops—the only crop
category for which yields are higher in the tropical countries than in
nontropical ones—contribute just 10 percent of food calories and only
3 percent of protein.

The same pattern of differential agricultural productivity appears
within Latin America, even though the region's countries are more
similar to one another than to the rest of the world. For most crops,
yields in tropical Latin American countries are much lower, although

Table 1.3 Per Capita Food Supply by Product
(percent)

Product	World Calories	World Protein	Central America Calories
Total	100	100	100
Vegetable products	84	63	84
Cereals (milled rice equivalent)	50	45	47
Wheat	20	22	9
Rice (milled equivalent)	21	15	3
Maize	5	5	34
Other	3	4	1
Root crops (potato, cassava, etc.)	5	3	1
Sugars	9	0	16
Pulses (beans and peas)	2	5	4
Oilcrops and oils	10	3	10
Vegetables	2	4	1
Fruits	3	1	3
Alcoholic beverages	2	0	2
Other	1	1	0
Animal products	16	37	16
Meat and animal fats	9	18	9
Milk, eggs, fish	6	19	7

Note: Totals may not equal the sum of their components because of rounding.
Source: Food and Agriculture Organization of the United Nations (1999).

Table 1.4 Average Crop Yields in Tropical versus
Nontropical Latin American Countries, 1998

Crop	Tropical yield (mt/ha)[a]	Nontropical yield (mt/ha)[a]	Tropical/ nontropical	Statistically significant difference[b]
Cereals (milled rice equivalent)	22.9	33.8	0.68	x
Maize	24.6	51.4	0.48	x
Root crops (potato, cassava, etc.)	122.0	218.0	0.56	x
Sugar cane[c]	700.0	632.0	1.11	
Pulses (beans and peas)	7.5	10.4	0.72	x
Oilcrops	6.2	5.3	1.17	
Vegetables	143.0	161.0	0.89	
Fruits	135.0	142.0	0.95	
Bananas	166.0	214.0	0.78	
Coffee	7.1	6.1	1.16	
Observations[d]	33	7		

a. Metric tons per hectare.

b. x = p value less than 5 percent for t test that mean tropical yield is different from mean nontropical yield.

c. Data are for 1996.

d. This is the number of countries with data for cereals. Not all countries produce root crops.

Source: Food and Agriculture Organization of the United Nations (1999).

none of the yield differences between the tropics and nontropics for these crops are statistically significant (see table 1.4).

Technological developments have also favored nontropical agriculture in Latin America. While there has been rapid growth of crop yields in the region for most staple crops, the growth rates are quite different between tropical and nontropical regions (see table 1.5). Although the yields of a few crops (coffee, fruits, vegetables, and oilcrops) grew slightly faster in the tropical countries, the largest improvements took place in the nontropical countries. Furthermore, the only statistically significant differences in productivity over the past 37 years favored the nontropical countries. It is no coincidence that the most successful exporters of agriculture-based goods in Latin America are nontropical countries. Chile has made great advances since the 1970s in the production of fruits for international markets

Table 1.5 Growth in Average Crop Yields in Tropical versus
Nontropical Latin American Countries, 1961–98

Crop	Tropical yield growth (%)	Nontropical yield growth (%)	Tropical/ nontropical	Statistically significant difference[a]
Cereals (milled rice equivalent)	1.8	2.6	−0.8	x
Maize	1.8	3.1	−1.3	x
Root crops (potato, cassava, etc.)	0.6	2.1	−1.5	x
Sugar cane[b]	0.8	1.0	−0.2	
Pulses (beans and peas)	0.3	0.6	−0.3	x
Oilcrops	2.0	1.8	0.2	
Vegetables	2.5	1.6	0.9	
Fruits	0.3	0.1	0.2	
Bananas	−0.3	0.2	−0.5	
Coffee	1.0	0.5	0.5	
Observations[c]	33.0	7.0		

a. x = p value less than 5 percent for t test that mean tropical yield growth is different from mean nontropical yield growth.

b. Data are for 1961–96.

c. This is the number of observations for cereals. Not all countries produce root crops.

Source: Food and Agriculture Organization of the United Nations (1999).

because it has taken advantage of technological developments in California, a region with which it shares some important geographical and ecological similarities (in addition to the advantage of the opposite pattern of seasons); this has been documented by Meller (1995, 1996).

The diet in Latin America, especially in the tropical countries, is different from other parts of the world. If the crops eaten by people in tropical Latin American countries were relatively more productive in the tropics, the yield differences between the tropics and nontropics for other crops would be less of a problem. The last column of table 1.3 shows that Central Americans eat much more maize, sugar, and pulses, which make up 54 percent of their calorie consumption compared to only 16 percent for the rest of the world. However, maize and beans are among the least productive crops in the tropics compared to the nontropics, both in Latin America and worldwide.[7]

Health Conditions

The relationship between physical geography and development extends beyond land productivity or the quality and availability of natural resources. Tropical regions are also poorer because of a heavier burden of disease. Geographical factors affect health conditions through many channels. The range and intensity of many diseases, particularly vector-borne ones, vary with climate. Malaria, hookworm, and schistosomiasis, in particular, are great debilitators that have been relatively easy to control in temperate zones but still defy major control efforts in the tropics. The lack of seasons makes control efforts more difficult because reproduction of the vectors of transmission takes place rather evenly throughout the year (see chapter 2 for an analysis of the seasonal patterns of vector- and water-borne diseases in Brazil). The allocation of technological investments has only reinforced the relative difficulty of controlling diseases typical of poorer areas, for the simple reason that those suffering from these diseases are too poor to pay for the vaccines or treatments, even if they have been developed or are available. Finally, and very important, policies and institutions may have reproduced differential health outcomes originally due to geography. European colonizers implanted better institutions in those colonies that enjoyed benign climates, where they expected to settle permanently, and resorted to more exploitative and less constructive systems of government where health conditions were harsher. The legacy of those original institutions may still be affecting the quality of government and the provision of public services in the former colonies.[8]

As a result, mortality is higher and life is shorter in the tropics. Latin American infant mortality rates peak in the tropics (see figure 1.8) and decline more or less continually to either side of the peak. The highest rates in the 10°–20° south are more than double the rate in the southern temperate zone, and 50 percent higher than that in the northern temperate zone. Life expectancy shows a similar pattern. Figure 1.9 shows that inhabitants of the temperate northern and southern ends of Latin America can expect to live about 75 years, but the trend line sags markedly in the tropical middle, dropping to 65 just south of the equator. The very low average lifespans of below 60 in provinces of Bolivia and Peru, and in Haiti, are all in the tropics. The two provinces close to the equator with life expectancies above 75 years are also in Peru: the capital Lima and its sister department of Callao, a clear sign of regional disparities within the country.

Since we have already seen that per capita income is lower in the tropics than in the temperate zones of Latin America, perhaps poor health in the tropics is simply due to poverty, not direct geographical

Figure 1.8 Infant Mortality by Latitude Band

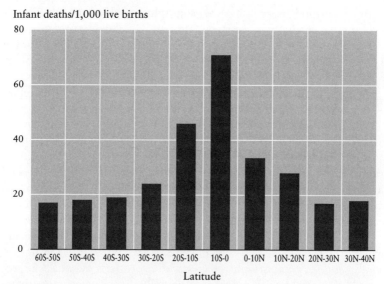

Source: World Bank (1998) and Environmental Systems Research Institute (1996).

Figure 1.9 Life Expectancy in Latin America by Latitude, 1995

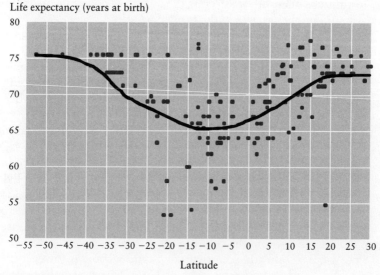

Sources: United Nations (1996), with subnational data from Alves and others (2000), Bitrán, Má, and Ubilla (2000), Escobal and Torero (2000), Esquivel (1999), Sánchez and Núñez (2000), and Urquiola and others (1999).

influences. After all, Bolivia and Haiti have the lowest life expectancy and are also poor countries. However, life expectancy is also short in tropical countries that on average are less poor, like Peru. If we are concerned with life expectancy as a measure of human welfare, it does not matter much whether climate affects it directly or indirectly through economic development—the fact remains that welfare is lower in the tropics. If the goal is to improve health conditions, however, it matters a great deal whether the most effective approach is to curtail the transmission of disease directly, or to invest resources in economic growth that will solve the health problems indirectly.

Climate and Health

Even after controlling for the influence of income levels, provincial life expectancy in Latin America is still correlated with climate. This suggests that climate affects health not only through income. One of the most robust correlates of health status is the education of mothers. When the influence of female literacy on health is included along with income levels, it is large and significant, and income loses its independent association with life expectancy.[9] Climate, however, is still strongly correlated with health outcomes. Controlling for female literacy and GDP per capita, life expectancy is four years lower in the wet tropics than in the humid temperate zone. These regression results, which are summarized in table 1.6, predict that life expectancy is seven years lower in the wet tropics than in desert and dry regions with the same income and female literacy. Similar results pertain to infant mortality (which is a component of life expectancy). Infant mortality is 4 percent higher in the wet tropics than in humid temperate regions, and 6 percent higher than in dry regions, other factors being equal.

One of the most conspicuous differences between the disease environment in tropical areas and that in temperate areas is malaria. Only in tropical areas of the world does malaria remain a major and intractable health problem. Map 1.7 (p. 25) shows the distribution of malaria in Latin America at three points in time: 1946, 1966, and 1994. Although malaria prevalence has been reduced, its core tropical zones resist control. Malaria is strongly related to climate, and there is no indication that it is affected by income levels or by female literacy (see table 1.6).

Natural Disasters

Although agricultural productivity and health conditions are the two main channels through which geography affects economic develop-

Table 1.6 Geography and Health, 1995

Independent variable	[1] Life expectancy (years at birth)	[2] Infant mortality rate (infant deaths/ 1,000 live births)	[3] Falciparum malaria index 1994 (0–1)
Log GDP per capita (PPP)	0.416	0.024	−0.014
	(0.64)	(0.01)	(0.42)
Female literacy rate (%)	0.286	−1.452	0.000
	(9.29)***	(7.66)***	(0.24)
Tropical, wet (%)	−4.332	40.722	0.275
	(4.01)***	(4.88)***	(5.22)***
Tropical, monsoon (%)	0.882	3.999	−0.019
	(1.45)	(0.61)	(0.09)
Tropical, some dry (%)	0.850	5.354	0.083
	(1.20)	(1.04)	(2.78)***
Dry steppe (%)	3.210	−18.505	−0.011
	(2.14)**	(2.27)**	(0.72)
Desert (%)	2.481	3.724	−0.012
	(4.27)***	(1.14)	(0.81)
Temperate, dry summer (%)	3.729	−8.720	0.000
	(3.69)***	(1.36)	(0.00)
Temperate, dry winter (%)	−3.557	26.959	−0.049
	(2.78)***	(1.59)	(1.34)
High elevation and polar (%)	−0.769	3.651	0.012
	(0.89)	(0.77)	(0.26)
Constant	41.716	156.385	0.165
	(8.79)***	(4.68)***	(0.42)
Observations	178	178	139
R^2	0.64	0.49	0.26

Note: GDP = gross domestic product, PPP = purchasing power parity values.
Robust t statistics are in parentheses.
    **Significant at 5%.
    ***Significant at 1%.

ment in Latin America and worldwide, many countries suffer continuous setbacks to their development efforts because of frequent and devastating natural disasters.

Latin America has suffered a disproportionate number of natural disasters during its recent history. Natural disasters are defined as natural events whose impact in terms of injuries, homelessness, fatalities, and destruction of assets creates severe economic and social hardship. There were 1,309 natural disasters in Latin America and the Caribbean between 1900 and 1999, accounting for 19 percent of reported disasters worldwide, behind only Asia, with 44 percent (Office of Foreign

Disaster Assistance 1999).[10] Between 1970 and 1999, the region was affected by 972 disasters—that is, more than 32 disasters a year on average—that are estimated to have killed 227,000 people, left about 8 million homeless, and otherwise affected almost 148 million people (see table 1.7). The annual average cost of these disasters over the past 30 years is estimated at between $700 million and $3.3 billion.[11]

The acute vulnerability of the region to natural disasters is the result of a combination of geographical and socioeconomic factors. Risks associated with natural events are a function of the magnitude of the physical phenomenon, frequency of occurrence, and the extent to which populations are vulnerable. All three elements are crucial to explaining why Latin America has suffered and continues to suffer significantly from natural disasters.

Location is the primary explanation for Latin America's vulnerability. The region is extremely prone to both earthquakes and volcano eruptions because its territory sits atop five active tectonic plates (Caribbean, Cocos, Nazca, Scotia, and South American plates). Part of the Pacific coast of South America is located along the Pacific "ring of fire," where 80 percent of the earth's seismic and volcanic activity takes place. Countries with the highest seismological risk include Mexico, which experienced 84 earthquakes measuring more than 7 on the Richter scale during the 20th century (World Bank 1999) as well as Chile, Colombia, Costa Rica, Ecuador, Guatemala, and Peru.

There is also extreme climatic volatility in the form of severe droughts, floods, and high winds in Latin America and the Caribbean due to the recurrent El Niño phenomenon,[12] the annual north-south displacement of the Inter-Tropical Convergence Zone, and the passage of tropical storms and hurricanes born in the Pacific and Atlantic Oceans. Traditional zones of high climatic volatility include Central America, the Caribbean, Northeast Brazil, Peru, Ecuador, Chile, and Argentina. Recent climatic changes seem to have aggravated climate volatility in the region.[13] Proponents of the climate change theory suggest that the impact of climate change in Latin America and the Caribbean would be an increase in intensity of heavy rainfall and more frequent and intense El Niño phenomena leading to floods on the west coast of Central and South America. Moreover, a further increase in the earth's temperature would contribute to a rising sea level, endangering coastal zones by making them much more vulnerable to surge flooding in the event of storms or hurricanes.

The region's overall vulnerability to natural disasters is not only determined by location and climate but also by various socioeconomic factors that greatly magnify the lethal and destructive potential of these events. These include patterns of settlements (particularly in vul-

Table 1.7 Major Natural Disasters in Latin America and the
Caribbean, 1970–2002

Year	Country	Disaster	Killed	Affected	Damages 1998 US$ (million)
1970	Brazil	Drought	—	10,000,000	0.4
1970	Peru	Earthquake	66,794	3,216,240	2,225.0
1972	Nicaragua	Earthquake	10,000	720,000	3,293.7
1973	Honduras	Landslide	2,800	0	—
1974	Honduras	Hurricane Fifi	8,000	730,000	1,784.6
1975	Brazil	Cold wave	70	600	1,817.0
1976	Guatemala	Earthquake	23,000	4,993,000	2,864.0
1978	Brazil	Drought	—	—	5,746.5
1979	Dom. Republic	Hurricanes David and Frederick	1,400	1,554,000	336.8
1983	Argentina	Flood	0	5,830,000	1,636.6
1983	Argentina	Flood	0	250,000	1,309.3
1983	Brazil	Drought	20	20,000,000	—
1983	Peru	Flood	364	700,000	1,618.3
1984	Brazil	Flood	17	159,600	1,568.9
1984	Brazil	Flood	10	120,400	1,568.9
1985	Argentina	Flood	12	206,000	1,969.4
1985	Chile	Earthquake	180	1,482,275	2,272.4
1985	Colombia	Volcano Nevada del Ruiz	21,800	12,700	1,515.0
1985	Mexico	Earthquake	8,776	130,204	6,059.8
1986	El Salvador	Earthquake	1,000	770,000	2,231.0
1987	Colombia	Earthquake	1,000	—	7,168.4
1987	Ecuador	Tsunami	1,000	6,000	—
1987	Ecuador	Earthquake	4,000	227,000	1,003.6
1988	Brazil	Flood	289	3,020,734	1,378.4
1988	Jamaica	Hurricane Gilbert	49	810,000	1,378.4
1988	Mexico	Hurricane Gilbert	240	100,000	1,860.9
1988	St. Lucia	Hurricane Gilbert	45	—	1,378.4
1989	NA-Caribbean	Hurricane Hugo	42	33,790	4,706.2
1991	El Salvador	Earthquake	1,000	—	—
1993	Mexico	Tropical Storms Arlene and Beatriz	7	10,000	1,884.5
1994	Haiti	Tropical Storm Gordon	1,122	1,587,000	—
1995	Virgin Isl. (U.S.)	Hurricane Marilyn	8	10,000	1,604.6
1996	Mexico	Drought	0	—	1,247.1
1998	Argentina	El Niño flood	19	360,000	2,500.0
1998	Brazil	Drought	0	10,000,000	97.8
1998	Dom. Republic	Hurricane Georges	288	4,515,238	2,193.4
1998	Ecuador	El Niño flood	322	88,753	2,869.3
1998	Honduras	Hurricane Mitch	5,657	2,112,000	2,000.0
1998	Mexico	Flood	1,256	506,744	—

(Table continues on the following page.)

Year	Country	Disaster	Killed	Affected	Damages 1998 US$ (million)
1998	Nicaragua	Hurricane Mitch	2,447	868,228	1,000
1998	Peru	Flood	340	580,750	1,200.0
1999	Colombia	Earthquake	1,186	1,205,933	2,837.9
1999	Venezuela	Flood/debris flow	30,000	483,635	1,957.2
2001	Brazil	Drought	0	1,000,000	—
2001	El Salvador	Earthquake	844	1,329,806	—
2001	El Salvador	Earthquake	315	252,622	—
2002	Chile	Flood	233	199,511	—

— Not available.

Source: EM-DAT: The OFDA/CRED International Disaster Database—www.cred. be/emdat—Université Catholique de Louvain, Brussels, Belgium.

nerable areas), the poor quality of housing and infrastructure, environmental degradation, the lack of efficient risk mitigation strategies, and types of economic activities.

High population density in disaster-prone areas contributes significantly to Latin America's vulnerability to disasters. Overall population density has increased due to demographic growth, resulting in a larger population vulnerable to natural disasters. The Latin American and Caribbean region has had rapid demographic growth in the last three decades, amounting to roughly 70 percent between 1970 and 1999. Today, with a total of 511.3 million inhabitants, the region has an average population density of 26 hab/km^2 (or about 65 inhabitants per square mile; United Nations Population Fund 1999). High-density zones (see figure 1.6) resulting from urbanization and migratory patterns are often located on the coasts and close to seismic faults. In Peru, the proportion of residents now living in coastal areas—within 80 kilometers (50 miles) of the sea—more susceptible to El Niño and other phenomena is 73 percent, compared to only 54 percent three decades ago (International Federation of the Red Cross 1999, p. 88).

Rapid urbanization has amplified the adverse consequences of natural disasters on economic activity and populations. By nature, cities are more physically and economically vulnerable to natural disasters because of the concentration of people and assets and the high degree of dependence of the inhabitants on urban networks of energy, water, and food distribution (Clarke 2000, p. 7). In addition, many cities are located in high-risk areas. At least two of the largest and fastest growing cities in Latin America—Mexico City and Lima—are located in zones with high seismic activity. The Mexico City earthquake in 1985 caused 8,700 fatalities and $4 billion in damages (Office of Foreign Disaster Assistance 1999). Lima has been badly damaged or destroyed by six earthquakes since 1856. Since 1940, the date of the last major earthquake, its population has increased sixfold, reaching 8.5 million. The risk of a major earthquake in Lima over the next 100 years has been estimated at 96 percent (International Federation of the Red Cross 1993, pp. 48–50).

Furthermore, because of rapid demographic growth and rural-urban migration, most cities have expanded without proper city planning, building codes, or land use regulations adapted to their geographical environment. Given a rate of urbanization of above 76 percent, an estimated 90 million Latin Americans in the year 2000 lived in urban areas (International Federation of the Red Cross 1993, p. 44). Cities in the region are particularly vulnerable to earthquakes and floods because of narrow streets, adobe or dry stone construction, and a lack of paved roads and green spaces. Migration to cities has increased demand for urban space and resulted in the expansion of poor neighborhoods on low-value terrain in risk-prone areas. Examples include the favelas on the slopes overlooking Rio de Janeiro, the shanty-towns of Guatemala City in ravines prone to landslides, and the slums of Tegucigalpa on flood plains and steep hillsides. Not surprisingly, city slums are usually the first neighborhoods—and sometimes the only ones—to be wiped out by natural disasters, as happened with the floods in Caracas in 1999 and Rio in 1988, and the 1976 earthquake in Guatemala City (Albala-Bertrand 1993, p. 93).

The poor quality of housing in the region, which also exacerbates the consequences of natural disasters, is primarily a result of rapid urbanization and widespread poverty. As of 1993, 37 percent of the total existing housing stock in Latin America provided inadequate protection against disaster and illness (Pan American Health Organization 1998). The Organization of American States (OAS) Caribbean Disaster Mitigation Project estimates that 60 percent of the total housing stock in the Caribbean is built without any technical input (International Federation of the Red Cross 1997, p. 80). Obviously, the poor quality of housing is closely linked to widespread poverty. In general, poor households lack the knowledge, technical skills, and income to deal with problems such as surface water drainage or the danger of collapse of dwellings built on the roofs of other dwellings. It has been reported that 40 percent of accidents in the favelas of Rio de Janeiro are caused by building collapses and another 30 percent by landslides (Hardoy 1989). Furthermore, the enforcement of building codes is weak in risk-prone areas, even in high-income neighborhoods, formal sector companies, and public infrastructure. On the Caribbean island of Montserrat, 98 percent of the housing collapses from the 1989 hurricane were due to noncompliance with wind and hurricane-resistant building codes. Damage totaled some $240 million, equal to five years of GDP (International Federation of the Red Cross 1997, p. 80).

Lagging investment in basic infrastructure also puts populations and assets at greater risk. As shown by the impact of Hurricane Mitch in Central America and El Niño in Peru and Ecuador, poor quality roads, bridges, airport, dams, and dikes are often destroyed during hurricanes and floods. This damage to infrastructure leads to higher numbers of fatalities, as well as wider and longer disruption of food distribution and economic activity. In the case of Hurricane Pauline in Mexico in 1997, half of the 400 fatalities were due to the inability to reach populations in isolated areas (Pan American Health Organization 1998). In Peru, total damage to infrastructure during the 1997–98 El Niño reached 5 percent of the country's GDP, causing a serious and long-lasting decline in several key economic sectors, including mining, the most important industry in the country (International Federation of the Red Cross 1999, p. 88). Similarly, the vulnerability of health infrastructure to disasters because of nondisaster-resilient building techniques and lack of maintenance decreases quality and access to care in the post-disaster emergency and recovery phase. In Mexico City, the modern wing of Juárez Hospital collapsed during the 1985 earthquake, causing many fatalities and paralyzing critical social infrastructure in a time of crisis (Pan American Health Organization and World Health Organization 1994, p. 72). Poorly designed and maintained potable water and waste management systems are also frequently damaged by disasters, increasing health risks such as cholera and leptospirosis.

The degradation of the environment also plays a crucial role in transforming natural events into disasters. Throughout the region, risk of flooding and landslides is exacerbated by deforestation of watersheds, the absence of soil conservation programs, and inappropriate land use. As a result of deforestation, the region lost 61 million hectares or 6 percent of its forest cover between 1980 and 1990. An additional 5.8 million hectares or 3 percent of the remaining total cover was lost between 1990 and 1995 (United Nations Environment Programme 2000, p. 123). Environmental degradation in the region is the result of higher population density in fragile ecosystems, as well as destructive agricultural activities. Instead of relying on more traditional and environment friendly cultivation techniques (such as terracing hillsides or planting crops in soil secured by roots of trees), the Latin American agricultural sector often uses methods that lead to widespread deforestation and erosion of soils. These in turn increase vulnerability to floods, drought, and landslides.

Most countries in the region still do not have efficient risk management policies in place. Agencies in charge of risk mitigation and preparedness are grossly underfunded relative to the costs of the risks from which they are supposed to protect the population. According to the Coordination Center for the Prevention of Natural Disasters (CEDEPRENAC; 1999, p. 13), none of the governments of Central America allocate enough resources from their national budgets for natural hazard management. Despite their proven efficiency, essential risk mitigation activities such as drainage, flood control, and reforestation of watersheds are sparse in risk-prone areas. Though equally important for risk reduction, land use regulation and building codes are rarely enforced. Furthermore, most lifeline infrastructure, such as hospitals, utilities, and airports, lacks proper emergency contingency plans. Finally, early warning, evacuation, and shelter systems do not cover all risk-prone areas and remain largely disorganized. Much of the mortality associated with Tropical Storm Gordon in Haiti in 1994 and Hurricane Cesar in 1996 in Costa Rica has been attributed to deficiencies or flaws in local warning and evacuation systems (Pan American Health Organization 1998).

In addition to being physically vulnerable to natural disasters, Latin American and Caribbean countries are also economically vulnerable. The macroeconomic impact of natural disasters mainly depends on the degree of vulnerability of exposed assets, the importance of the economic activities affected, and the impact of these activities on other sectors and public finances. In severe disasters, losses can reach or exceed 10 percent of a country's GDP and reduce GDP growth during one to three years. The economic impact also depends on macroeconomic conditions before the disaster, the degree of diversification of the economy, and the size of financial and insurance markets. Finally, the amount, timing, and price of the contingent financing available for reconstruction will affect the final macroeconomic outcome. The lack of sectoral diversification in the region helps to explain why natural disasters have a significant adverse impact on the aggregate level. Agriculture, which is directly linked with climatic conditions, is still a key sector in terms of its share of GDP and employment. The weight of the agricultural sector in rural areas, coupled with the absence of alternative occupational options, creates greater risks of massive unemployment, income loss, and recession in areas with high climatic volatility. In Honduras, the country hardest hit by Hurricane Mitch, and where direct damages represented 38 percent of the country's GDP, 77.6 percent of productive sector losses were concentrated in agriculture, livestock, and fisheries. This sector represents 20 percent of GDP, 63 percent of exports, and 50 percent of total employment. As a result of Mitch, activity in the agricultural sector contracted by 8.7 percent in 1999 and real GDP growth was −2 percent (Economist Intelligence

Unit 2000, pp. 24 and 34; Economic Commission for Latin America and the Caribbean 1999, p. 78; International Monetary Fund 2000).

The limited capacity of insurance and reinsurance markets also makes the region more vulnerable to natural disasters by preventing risk pooling and burden sharing. Munich Re, a major reinsurance company, estimates that between 1985 and 1999, the amount of damages covered by insurance in Latin America and the Caribbean was $420 million, that is, only 3.8 percent of total damages (Münchener Rück 2000, pp. 64–65). El Niño caused $2.8 billion in damage to public infrastructure in Peru, of which only $150 million was insured (International Federation of the Red Cross 1999, p. 97). It is therefore left to the state, companies, and individuals to absorb the bulk of the shock created by the destruction of physical capital and the decline in economic activity.

Access to Markets

For economic development, access to the main world markets is crucial. Only world markets provide the scale, degree of competition, and access to technological and organizational changes needed to efficiently produce most goods. Access to world markets depends on the factors that determine the cost of seaborne transport—the distance of the country from principal world markets, and whether the bulk of economic activity is located close to the coast or a large, navigable river.

Why are these factors so important? For most goods, the world markets are dominated by a relatively small number of industrial countries in Europe and North America and by Japan. Proximity to these regions is a substantial economic advantage. For the few developing countries that have in fact enjoyed rapid economic growth over the past generation, the export of labor-intensive manufactures has played a prominent role. Trade in these goods depends largely on seaborne transport. But since the actual cost of transport is but a fraction of the value of the final goods, why do transport costs have such a significant economic impact? When investment goods are imported, as they almost always are outside of the most prosperous countries, transport costs serve as a tax on investment that varies depending on the country's accessibility. If the inputs to production are also imported, as they usually are in export manufactures, the impact of this tax is greatly magnified (this is shown formally in Gallup, Sachs, and Mellinger 1999). It is not unusual in offshore assembly manufacturing for the value of inputs to be 70 percent of the value of the finished export. If shipping costs are 10 percent of the value of the goods shipped, applied to both the imported inputs and the exported finished good, transport costs make up a remarkable 56 percent of the domestic value added.[14] If transport costs are half this rate, at 5 percent, then the ratio of shipping costs to value added falls to 25 percent. Such a difference in transport costs is often enough to render the higher shipping cost to a more distant location entirely unprofitable.

Access to the sea is as important for economic accessibility as is distance from international markets, if only because overland transport costs are much higher than sea shipping, especially in poor countries with limited infrastructure. The cost of shipping goods overland within a country can be as high as the cost of shipping them by sea to a far-flung foreign port.[15] Almost all countries with macroeconomic success in labor-intensive manufacturing exports have populations almost completely within 100 kilometers (about 62 miles) of the coast.

From the point of view of access to markets, the countries of the Caribbean basin are ideally situated. They are close to the large U.S. market, and most of their populations and economic activities take place near coastlines. With conductive trade policies and complementary infrastructure, Caribbean and Central American countries should have a competitive advantage over the more successful East Asian export manufacturers. Why would U.S. firms go all the way across the Pacific to take advantage of low wages for manufacturing assembly if educated, low-wage workers are only a couple of hundred miles away?

Trade policies in the Caribbean and the development of export processing zones (EPZs) have started to take advantage of this potential. The role of EPZs as a stepping stone to the development of an export manufacturing sector highlights the importance of coastal access. As shown in map 1.8 (p. 26) and table 1.8, 152 of the 210 export processing zones in Latin America and the Caribbean in 1997 were located within 100 kilometers of the coast. Most of the inland EPZs are

Table 1.8 Access to the Sea by Latin American Export Processing Zones

Indicator	Coastal	Noncoastal
Export processing zones	152	58
Percent of all EPZs	72	28
EPZs excluding Mexico and Bolivia	112	7
Percent of all EPZs	94	6

Note: Includes free trade and maquiladora zones. Coastal sites are within 100 kilometers of the sea coast. Many EPZ locations in map 1.8 (p. 26) have more than one export processing zone.

Source: World Economic Processing Zones Association (1997).

Figure 1.10 Difference in Growth between Mexican Border
States and the Rest of Mexico

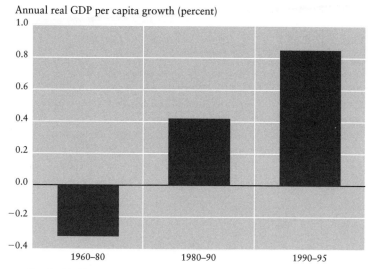

Annual real GDP per capita growth (percent)

Source: Esquivel (1999).

in northern and central Mexico, with good overland access to the U.S.
market, and in landlocked Bolivia. Excluding Mexican and Bolivian
EPZs, 112 of 119 EPZs, or 94 percent, are on the coast.

Caribbean and Central American economies are benefiting from
deepening trade ties with the United States, while many South American countries are currently facing economic crises. Economic performance within Mexico shows this trend. Per capita GDP growth in the
Mexican states that border the United States grew 0.3 percent slower
than the other Mexican states from 1960 to 1980, when the economy
was largely closed to external trade (see figure 1.10). With trade liberalization in the 1980s opening the economy to the U.S. market, growth
in the border states was 0.4 percent *faster* than the other states (though
the country as a whole had declining GDP per capita. Over 1990–95,
with the advent of the North American Free Trade Agreement
(NAFTA), the northern border states grew 0.8 percent faster than the
rest of the states, despite the continuing decline in overall GDP per
capita.

Other Latin American countries are less favored than Mexico or the
Central American and Caribbean countries in terms of their access to
markets. Bolivia and Paraguay are landlocked, which reduces their
trade possibilities. Despite Colombia's access to the Atlantic and the
Pacific, the bulk of the country's economic activities are located in the

Andean mountains, where climate conditions are more benign but access is difficult. Until recently, the country even lacked good roads to connect its main regions. Roads in Colombia up until the 20th century connected villages only within each region, with no roads across regions. As late as 1930, the main link from the capital of Bogota to the outside world was a 12-day steamboat trip down the Magdalena River. Because of its geographical barriers, Colombia still has one of the lowest road densities in Latin America. Despite recent trade liberalization, the country's economic activity is still concentrated in and around Bogota.

The importance of geographical barriers and problems of location can change over time. The lowlands of landlocked Bolivia, for example, have experienced a major boom over the last two decades due to the combination of new road connections and expanded trade opportunities with neighboring countries. Of course, the location of cities can still be a major obstacle to exploiting these new opportunities, especially when a country's largest city is home to a very large proportion of the population, as is usually the case in Latin America.

Urban Primacy in Latin America

Development and urbanization have moved together at least since the dawn of the industrial revolution in the 19th century. Urbanization has brought advantages to many people, from better sanitary conditions to higher wages. Still, there is not a unique path of urbanization. The size and distribution of cities vary widely from one country to another. While in some countries urban residents tend to agglomerate around one large city, in others they may be spread over several cities, both large and small. These differences affect development outcomes in various and complex ways, as long recognized by urban economists and other social scientists.

Urbanization has most often been accompanied by the concentration of population in one primary city. This process of urban concentration, once limited to industrial countries, has recently become a staple feature of many developing countries, especially in Africa and Latin America. Figure 1.11 shows that urban concentration, or the percentage of the urban population living in a country's main city, is larger today in Latin America than in any region of the world. Only Sub-Saharan Africa has levels that are even comparable, but with much lower urban populations. Figure 1.12 shows that Latin America's preeminence in terms of urban concentration is no recent phenomenon. As far back as the 1950s, average urban concentration

Figure 1.11 Urban Concentration around the World
in the 1990s

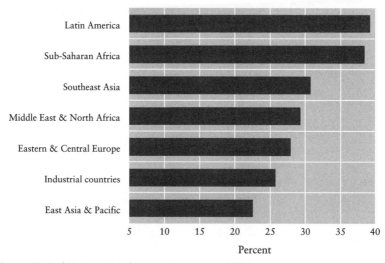

Source: United Nations Development Programme (1996).

Figure 1.12 Urban Concentration in Latin America and the
Rest of the World, 1950–90

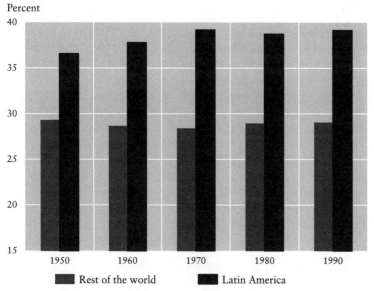

Source: United Nations Development Programme (1996).

in Latin America was 6 percentage points larger than that of the rest of the world. This difference grew somewhat in the 1960s and 1970s and has since remained stable.

Within Latin America, the process of urban concentration has varied from country to country. Differences across countries are evident in Figure 1.13, not only in levels of urban concentration but also in how it has progressed over time. Current urban concentration ranges from around 15 percent in Brazil to more than 65 percent in Panama. While the range of variation has remained stable, the evolution of urban concentration has differed widely from one country to the next. Thus, some countries show steady increases in urban concentration (Chile, Colombia, El Salvador, Haiti, Nicaragua, and Peru), some countries persistent declines (Argentina, Uruguay, and Venezuela), and others stable patterns (Brazil and Ecuador).

The levels of urban concentration are associated with some basic country characteristics in predictable ways. Gaviria and Stein (1999) show that urban concentration is lower in smaller countries (it drops by 1 percentage point for every million square kilometers, or approximately 385,000 square miles), and lower in richer countries (it drops by 1 percentage point for every $1,000 per capita). On average, urban

Figure 1.13 Urban Concentration in Latin America, 1950 and 1990

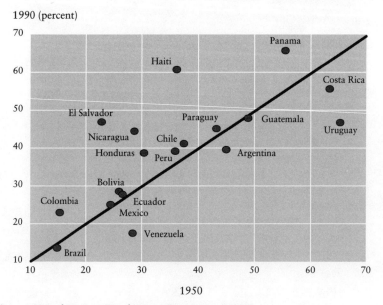

Source: United Nations Development Programme (1996).

concentration is 10 percentage points higher in countries where the primary city is also the capital and 2 percentage points higher in countries where the primary city is a port.

The changes in urban concentration are also affected by country characteristics. The few studies that have examined the effects of political and economic variables show that urban concentration grows faster in politically unstable regimes and more volatile economies, and slower in more open economies, especially if the main city is landlocked.[16]

The most conspicuous effect of urban concentration is the emergence of giant cities. Giant cities have long terrorized urban planners who cannot understand why people insist, against their admonitions, to live there. By contrast, urban giants fascinate urban economists who have long suspected that people live there for a reason. Urban giants are riddled with problems and full of possibilities.

Urban giants suffer from a long list of maladies, from higher pollution to more traffic congestion and longer commuting times. In Los Angeles, for example, more than 2.3 million person-hours are lost to traffic delay in a typical year (see Gleick 1999). In all likelihood, these numbers are even higher in many cities in the developing world, from

Figure 1.14 Interpersonal Trust and City Size in Latin America

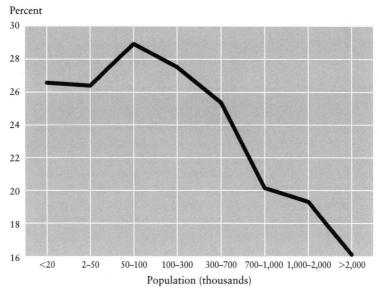

Source: Latinobarómetro (system of opinion surveys that covers 17 countries), various years.

São Paulo to Bangkok. Urban giants (and large cities in general) also suffer from higher crime rates, although these appear to level off once cities reach population levels over 1 million (see box 1.4). Moreover, larger cities have lower levels of social capital (from weaker community ties to lower interpersonal trust). Figure 1.14 shows, for example, that the proportion of people who report trusting others falls sharply with city size in Latin America.

Box 1.4 Crime and the City

In Latin America and the world in general, crime is much worse in urban areas than rural ones, and within urban areas, much worse in large cities than small ones. Although this connection is rarely quantified, it is already part of the collective unconscious: our bands of criminals are no longer found in desolate landscapes in the countryside, but in the heart of large cities, among tall skyscrapers and impassive pedestrians (based on Gaviria and Pagés 2002).

Several hypotheses have been suggested for explaining the positive association between crime and city size. One possibility is that large cities present better victims: their inhabitants are wealthier and generally have more goods that can be stolen and disposed of. Another possibility is that people with a greater propensity to become criminals are overly concentrated in large cities, whether because the urban environment favors criminal behavior or because young men or other high-risk groups are more disproportionately likely to migrate to cities. Yet another possibility is that those who violate the law are less likely to be arrested (and sentenced) in large cities, either because of the existence of "declining yields" in producing arrests, or because large cities—usually overwhelmed with all kinds of needs—do not invest enough in police and the justice system, or even because there is less cooperation with law enforcement in urban areas.

The purpose here is more descriptive than analytical: rather than sorting out the hypotheses mentioned above, the objective is simply to establish to what extent there is a positive connection between city size and the prevalence of crime in Latin America. This is not easy, since crime statistics are scarce, and when they do exist, they are rarely comparable between countries.

Fortunately, the Latinobarómetro survey system can be used to study the correlation between crime and city size. This system offers several advantages. In particular, it provides comparable information on crime rates (victimization in this instance) for 17 countries in the region and, even more important, for many cities in the interior of each country. Latinobarómetro provides information on victimization rates for more than 80 cities in Latin America, including all the region's large cities.

Figure 1.15 City Size and Victimization in Latin America

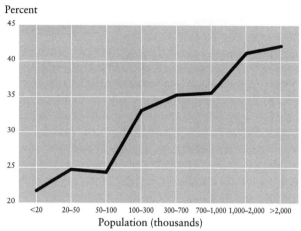

Source: Gaviria and Pagés (2002).

Figure 1.15 shows the pattern of change in victimization rates vis-à-vis city size. The relationship is clearly a rising one, although it is not exactly linear. (Victimization rates measure the proportion of families who report that at least one of their members was the victim of some crime during the most recent 12 months.) In general, three groups of cities can be distinguished: a first group made up of cities of under 100,000 inhabitants, which on average have low crime rates; a second group with between 100,000 and 1 million inhabitants, where crime rates are intermediate; and a third group with populations of over 1 million inhabitants, which have high crime rates.

Gaviria and Pagés (2002) show that the positive association between criminality and population occurs not only in the aggregate but also, and without exception, in each country in Latin America by itself. Something similar can be seen if one analyzes other sources of information and other regions of the world. Figures 1.16 and 1.17 show, for example, that the association between victimization and city size is quite strong in Colombia and is clearly apparent in the United States.

Gaviria and Pagés also show that there is a positive correlation between criminality and population growth. Hence, not only do large cities have more crime, cities that have grown more rapidly suffer from the same affliction. Naturally, in many instances, population growth is faster in the largest cities, which keep absorbing new inhabitants while helplessly watching crime and violence increase.

(Box continues on the following page.)

Box 1.4 (continued)

Figure 1.16 City Size and Victimization in the United States

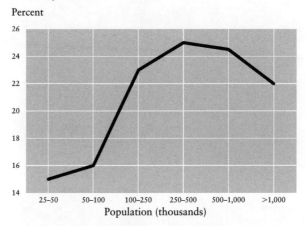

Source: Glaeser and Sacerdote (1996).

Figure 1.17 City Size and Victimization in Colombia

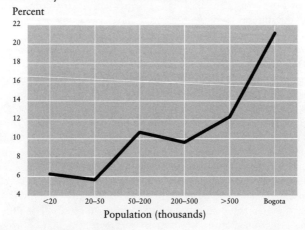

Source: Gaviria and Pagés (2002).

Box 1.4 (continued)

It is quite difficult, if not impossible, for lack of information to directly examine the hypotheses mentioned above regarding the positive association between crime and city size. However, some evidence seems to run counter to the first two hypotheses (more victims in large cities or greater percentages of potential criminals). Gaviria and Pagés find that the positive association between crime and city size remains even after controlling for the wealth of inhabitants and the social and economic characteristics of cities. This would not be the case if large cities had more crime due to the presence of more and better victims or the presence of a greater proportion of individuals at a higher risk of committing crimes (young men, migrants, or youth who are not part of the education system).

Latin American cities today face many challenges: they must not only deal with growing demands for public services and infrastructure but must also ensure citizen safety in an ever more complicated setting. There are no easy answers to the problem of urban violence. But it is clear that investment must be made in policing, and the most obvious risk factors (alcohol and weapons) must be controlled. And it must also be kept in mind that once the forces driving crime gather momentum, they are hard to stop.

Further, the concentration of a country's economic activity in a single city can have deleterious consequences. Dominant primary cities are often forced to subsidize stagnant regions, and subsidies can in turn cause all kinds of distortions. Moreover, overly dominant primary cities can create resentment and exacerbate ethnic and racial conflicts.

Having summarized the negatives, it must also be said that their large size can bring benefits to cities and their residents as well. Large cities enjoy significant economies of scale in providing basic public services, including education and health. They also enjoy significant agglomeration economies, stemming from both knowledge spillovers within industries and cross-fertilization between industries. And finally, large cities give rise to large markets, which in turn facilitate the division of labor and reduce transport costs. All these forces certainly should make primal cities more productive, and, therefore, the focal points of any strategy to spur economic growth.[17]

Economic development in Latin America, then, will hinge heavily on the fates of primary cities. If primary cities are unable to harness their many possibilities and cope with their mounting problems, economic development will be very difficult, to say the least. Herein then lies one of the main challenges for the region in the years to come.

Will Geography Matter in the Future?

The previous sections have examined how the five channels of physical and human geography—agricultural productivity, health conditions, natural disasters, access to markets, and urbanization—can affect economic and social development. But these associations between development outcomes and geographical features may be due to *past* influences that no longer affect the potential for future improvement. So this section puts these strands together to assess whether or to what extent geography can be expected to matter in the future.

The first step in answering this question is obviously to control for the past and to establish, on the basis of recent experience worldwide, whether geography is still important to prospects for development. This requires selecting a set of simple indicators that synthesize the main channels of influence of geography, as shown in figure 1.18.

Figure 1.18 Geography Matters: Regional Differences

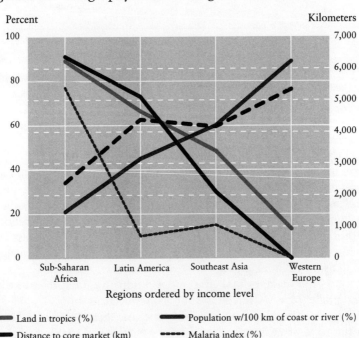

Sources: Environmental Systems Research Institute (1996), Tobler (1995), United Nations Development Programme (1996), and World Health Organization (1997).

The first indicator is tropical location, a proxy for land productivity and agriculture technological disadvantages, which is measured by the percent of the country's land area within the geographical tropics. Malaria prevalence, the second indicator, is a prime measure of the burden of disease caused by purely geographical factors. It is an index that weighs both the percentage of the population at risk for malaria and the percentage of the infected population that suffers from the most severe kind of malaria.[18] The third indicator reflects the proximity of countries in each region to core world markets by measuring the distance of the capital city in kilometers from Tokyo, New York, and Rotterdam. Fourth, within-country access to the sea is measured by the percentage of the population living within 100 kilometers of the coast or an ocean navigable river. For inland landlocked countries, this will be zero. Finally, urbanization is measured as the percentage of the population living in urban areas (as defined by each country; see United Nations Development Programme 1996).

These five simple indicators provide a good summary of the geographical advantages or disadvantages of each of the major regions of the world.[19] Latin America as a whole fares reasonably well when comparing its geographical endowments to the rest of the developing world. Countries in Latin America have good access to the sea, with the exceptions of Bolivia and Paraguay. The population is mostly concentrated on the coasts. The states bordering the Caribbean are all close to the large North American commercial market. Urbanization rates are high in most countries. Agriculture in the region benefits from large areas with temperate climate owing to latitude or elevation. Most vector-borne diseases, including malaria, do not have the virulence found in Africa.

This favorable geography accounts for Latin America having many of the higher income countries in the tropics worldwide. But whereas Latin America compares favorably in terms of geography and income levels with the rest of the developing world, it does not compare well on either count with highly industrialized countries in Europe and North America, nor with Japan or Australia. Further, the relationship of each of these geographical indicators with income levels does not make clear whether they will continue to be relevant to future economic development.

For example, income levels could well be affected by historical processes that depended on geography, while future economic growth would be largely independent of physical geography. The "new economic geography" espoused by Paul Krugman and others follows this line of reasoning (Fujita, Krugman, and Venables 1999). Locations with initial geographical advantages serve as catalysts for developing networks, but once the networks are established, physical geography ceases to have an impact on economic activity. The forces of agglomeration can create a differentiated economic geography even if there was little geographical variation in the first place.

The endogenous processes described in economic geography models reinforce and magnify the direct impact of physical geography and help to explain the dynamics of the process. Natural ports, for example, become focal points for the development of cities, which can become more dominant over time if the economies of agglomeration outweigh the costs of congestion. If these processes dominate, though, we are unlikely to find a strong relationship between geography and economic growth, once we have controlled for the initial conditions. Is it true, for instance, that Hong Kong and Singapore still depend on their excellent access to major shipping lanes for their economic success? Or was that just important to get them started? Is the disease burden in Africa just a reflection of the continent's poverty, perhaps due to the accident of colonization, or will it be an independent drag on African development because it is tied to the tropical climate?

To address the continuing relevance of geography to economic development, the rest of this section examines cross-country relationships of geographical variables to economic growth, controlling for other important determinants of growth, including initial conditions. This allows for measuring the impact of geographical factors for current economic growth prospects. The presentation that follows is nontechnical, but the more inquisitive reader may want to scrutinize the details, which are contained in table 1.9.

The Influence of Natural and Human Geography on Growth

We start with a baseline equation similar to those in Barro and Sala-i-Martin (1995), in which average income growth between 1965 and 1990 is a function of initial income in 1965, the initial level of education in 1965 (measured by average years of secondary school), the log of life expectancy at birth in 1965, the openness of the economy to international trade, and the quality of public institutions.[20] We find the standard results for these variables: conditional on other variables, poorer countries catch up by growing faster, and output is an increasing function of education, life expectancy, openness, and the quality of public institutions. We stress the fact that these results are conditional on other factors because, as we have seen, a large number of poorer countries do not grow faster than richer ones. As we will see below, this is due to a large extent to their unfavorable geographical conditions. To these variables we add different combinations of geographical variables, allowing us to test the consistency and robustness of the results. We find that the five basic indicators of physical and human geography described above consistently show the expected signs and are, in general, highly significant.

According to these results, countries fully located within the tropics grow around 0.3 percentage point less than nontropical countries. Although a simple estimate is nonsignificant, when tropicality is interacted with initial income levels, the results become very significant. The estimated coefficients imply that, all else being equal, a country fully located within the tropics that starts with a level of per capita income twice that of another tropical country will be able to grow around 0.7 percentage point faster. As intuition suggests, the limitations imposed by natural geography become less restrictive as countries become richer.[21] This is both good news and bad news, as it confirms that geography is not destiny—after all, there are also some rich countries in the tropics—but suggests that the initial effort required to break away from poverty is much harder for a tropical than for a nontropical country. A bigger push is required to take off in the tropics.

The results also give support to the hypothesis that health conditions related to geography may be a major obstacle to development. All else being equal, countries at high risk of malaria grow 0.6 percentage point slower than countries free from malaria. Such a large estimated impact of malaria on economic growth is striking, especially since the estimates control for general health conditions (life expectancy) and for a general tropical effect. The one country in the Americas with a malaria index of 1, Haiti, is also the poorest country in the hemisphere. A reduction in malaria could give Haiti and some other Latin American countries a big economic impulse.

There is some evidence that natural disasters may also affect growth. Although we lack an appropriate indicator for this influence of geography, an indicator of the mortality caused by earthquakes and volcanic eruptions between 1902 and 1996 is inversely and significantly associated with growth (after controlling for other main determinants of growth, including physical geographical variables). The problem with this variable is that it captures only some types of disasters, and the mortality due to a given natural disaster depends on the country's poverty, so it is not an independent cause of development. Therefore, it is excluded from other regressions.

The econometric evidence strongly supports the hypothesis that population settlement patterns have important implications for growth. Areas with populations located away from the coast experience lower rates of growth. The estimates also support the notion that

Table 1.9 Determinants of GDP per Capita Growth, 1965–90

Independent variable	[1]	[2]	[3]	[4]	[5]	[6]	[7]	[8]
Controls								
GDP per capita, 1965 (log)	−2.329	−2.533	−2.908	−2.878	−3.239	−2.880	−3.893	−3.994
	(−7.64)	(−7.28)	(−6.91)	(−7.02)	(−7.46)	(−5.65)	(−9.47)	(−10.20)
Years of secondary schooling, 1965 (log)	0.265	0.177	0.057	0.108	0.029	0.015	0.038	0.074
	(1.85)	(1.20)	(0.42)	(0.71)	(0.21)	(0.10)	(0.19)	(0.55)
Life expectancy, 1965 (log)	6.506	4.731	4.608	4.702	3.839	3.953	5.351	4.059
	(7.30)	(4.27)	(4.40)	(4.24)	(4.34)	(4.52)	(4.93)	(4.07)
Trade openness, 1965–90 (0–1)	1.889	1.795	2.110	1.864	1.866	1.950	1.590	1.587
	(5.47)	(4.58)	(5.15)	(5.02)	(3.97)	(4.03)	(3.01)	(3.58)
Institutional quality (0–1)	0.282	0.357	0.390	0.431	0.382	0.345	0.484	0.468
	(3.30)	(3.32)	(3.52)	(4.40)	(3.75)	(3.33)	(3.61)	(4.25)
Physical geography								
Share of land in tropics (0–1)		−0.333	−8.915	−8.311	−8.180	−5.842	−9.504	−10.681
		(−0.73)	(−2.86)	(−2.70)	(−2.86)	(−1.76)	(−3.41)	(−3.64)
Share of land in tropics times GDP per capita 1965			1.111	1.077	0.992	0.682	1.184	1.293
			(2.82)	(2.77)	(2.74)	(1.62)	(3.37)	(3.54)
Falciparum malaria index, 1965 (0–1)		−1.404	−0.902	−1.113	−0.602	−0.717	−0.650	−0.717
		(−2.39)	(−1.64)	(−2.05)	(−1.26)	(−1.43)	(−1.14)	(−1.19)
Earthquakes and volcanos index (0–1)				−1.651				
				(−3.06)				
Human geography								
Population urban, 1965 (percent)					2.249	1.457	2.290	2.471
					(2.86)	(1.71)	(2.70)	(3.46)

62

	(1)	(2)	(3)	(4)	(5)	(6)	(7)	(8)
Population within 100 km of coast (0–1)					0.602 (1.26)		2.710 (1.73)	1.977 (2.13)
Distance to main markets (log)					−5.90 (−1.08)	−2.93 (−0.48)	−7.29 (−1.16)	−6.85 (−1.17)
Coastal population density, 1994 (log)						0.170 (2.25)		
Inland population density, 1994 (log)						−0.087 (−1.19)		
Infrastructure								
Total road length, 1965 (log)							0.196 (1.22)	
Coastal population share times (log) road length							−0.244 (−1.50)	
Electricity generating capacity, 1965 (log)								0.220 (1.55)
Coastal population share times (log) electricity generating capacity								−0.223 (−1.93)
Constant	−8.792 (−2.92)	0.014 (0.003)	3.143 (0.75)	2.329 (0.53)	7.811 (2.11)	4.878 (1.11)	4.580 (0.96)	11.175 (2.43)
R^2	0.70	0.75	0.77	0.79	0.79	0.80	0.84	0.85
Observations	77	77	77	72	76	76	58	71

Note: GDP = gross domestic product. t statistics are in parentheses.
Source: Authors' calculations.

there are agglomeration effects from population concentrations on the coast, but diminishing returns to dense populations in the interior. Countries with high population density near the coast grow faster, and countries with high population density in the interior grow more slowly. The results suggest that distance to international markets also affects growth. In general, however, the precision of the estimates is rather low, and parameter estimates vary significantly from one specification to the other, suggesting that factors specific to each country may come into play.

Finally, the estimates strongly support the hypothesis that the economic benefits of urbanization outweigh the costs, allowing more urbanized countries to grow faster. All else being equal, a country that starts with a rate of urbanization 50 percentage points higher than another can be expected to grow at a rate about 1 percentage point higher. This also offers support to the big push thesis, but applied to the process of urbanization.

Geographical Influences on Differences in Growth between Regions

Table 1.10 shows the estimated impact of specific variables on differences in growth between Latin America, the industrial countries, and East Asia. Average growth of GDP per capita in Latin American countries over 1965–90 was 0.9 percent per year, less than half of the 2.7 percent growth rate of the countries in the Organisation for Economic Co-operation and Development (OECD), and much lower than East and Southeast Asia's dramatic 4.6 percent growth per year. The "total explained" row in the table shows the sum of the predicted contribution of the explanatory variables, and is quite close to the actual differences in the regional growth rates.

The first block of explanatory variables comprises controls that capture initial conditions (other than geography), policy, and institutional characteristics of the countries. These factors explain around a third of the growth gap of nearly 1.7 points between Latin America and the industrial countries, and 3.3 of the 3.8 points of growth difference between Latin America and the East Asian countries. Most of these differences come from the fact that policies and institutions have been less favorable to growth in Latin America than in these two groups of countries.

Geographical factors explain a large portion of the remaining growth gap between Latin America and the industrial countries, but not between Latin America and East Asia. The industrial countries enjoy more favorable physical and human geographical factors, each

Table 1.10 Decomposition of the Difference in GDP per Capita Growth between Latin America and Other Regions of the World, 1965–90

	With respect to	
Variable	Industrial countries	East Asia
Controls	0.564	3.293
GDP per capita, 1965 (log)	−3.499	1.404
Years of secondary schooling, 1965 (log)	0.025	0.008
Life expectancy, 1965 (log)	0.755	0.017
Trade openness, 1965–90 (0–1)	1.487	1.227
Institutional quality (0–1)	1.796	0.637
Physical geography	0.682	−0.519
Share of land in tropics		
(and its interaction with income)	0.594	−0.392
Falciparum malaria index, 1965 (0–1)	0.088	−0.127
Human geography	0.598	0.101
Percentage urban population, 1965	0.423	−0.042
Coastal population	−0.007	0.135
Distance to main markets	0.183	0.008
Total geography	1.280	−0.418
Total explained	1.844	2.875
Total observed	1.697	3.771
Unexplained	−0.147	0.895

Source: Authors' calculations based on regression [5] of table 1.9.

of which explains roughly a third of the growth gap. The main advantages of industrial countries stem from their location in temperate zones and their higher urbanization rates. Latin America and East Asia have rather similar geographical characteristics, and only a small fraction of the growth gap between the two regions can be attributed to geography. Furthermore, geographical factors would tend to make East Asia grow slightly less than Latin America. This point is crucial, because it reinforces the argument that geography is not destiny, and that adequate policies and institutions can offset its adverse effects.

At this point it is convenient to discuss how much of the dictum of geography can be offset by infrastructure policies. Although this question naturally pertains to chapter 3, where it will receive greater attention, we can take advantage of the econometric results just discussed to evaluate the impact of infrastructure on growth possibilities and to discuss whether it can counteract adverse geographical conditions.

In principle, infrastructure can help overcome many of the obstacles imposed by geography, but often at costs beyond the reach of poor countries. In areas where geography poses particularly difficult problems—such as mountainous regions, humid tropical zones where soils and torrential rains make it difficult to build durable roads, and regions far from the sea or without good natural ports—building such infrastructure is much more expensive than in coastal, temperate areas. Furthermore, those investments may be less productive than in better-endowed areas that support much more economic activity.

To see if infrastructure investment is less productive in geographically difficult environments, we examine whether infrastructure has a smaller impact on economic growth in countries with limited access to the coast. In landlocked countries, initial road stocks and initial electricity generation capacity are positively correlated with subsequent growth, but at low significance levels. In coastal countries, there is no significant effect of initial infrastructure on subsequent growth (after accounting for policies, institutions, and so forth). The results suggest that there might be some room to achieve better rates of return from infrastructure in noncoastal areas, but the effect is far from guaranteed. These weak associations may reflect the fact that the quality of investments is less determined by geographical conditions than by the quality of institutions and the extent of corruption.[22]

Geography has been and continues to be an important, but not insurmountable, obstacle to Latin America's development. This chapter has painted in broad brushstrokes the four faces of this relationship. But the picture is incomplete. The details, the nuances, indeed the exceptions that distinguish a snapshot from real life, are laid out in the case studies that follow in the subsequent chapter. These will provide further evidence that the influence of geography can be as variable as the weather itself.

Notes

1. However, human arrival in the Americas may have been as early as 25,000 B.C., although much debate surrounds these estimates.

2. Substantial evidence points to sustained drought brought on by the El Niño climatic oscillation as the cause of the Mayan collapse, due to high population density agriculture on fragile tropical soils; see Fagan (1999, chapter 8).

3. The lack of domesticable livestock in the Americas for use in agriculture as well as war was probably due to the impact of the first human settlers of the Americas 13,000 years ago on large mammals, ironically similar to the deadly impact of European settlers on the descendants of the original American

settlers. American mammals had no experience of coevolution with humans until the Asian migrants' sudden appearance, and thus no natural wariness and defenses against human attack. In the Americas, as in Australia, the first human settlers brought about the extinction of most of the large mammals; see Crosby (1986, pp. 273–81).

4. Although not included in figure 1.5, historical evidence shows that Haiti was France's richest colony and most likely had income levels similar to Cuba before the slave rebellion destroyed the plantations; see Heinl and Heinl (1978, p. 2).

5. Pricing and other agricultural policies have a substantial effect on how much farmers produce and the amount of inputs they use, but to a first approximation, should not affect yields given inputs.

6. For extensive analysis and documentation of this important point, see Diamond (1997).

7. One may wonder why people in Latin America eat relatively large shares of items that are unproductive, instead of adopting more cost-effective diets. Although this may be changing with the internationalization of these economies, diets still reflect ancient traditions and a legacy of policies aimed at isolating agricultural product markets from outside competition.

8. Forceful empirical evidence in support of this hypothesis is offered by Acemoglu, Johnson, and Robinson (2001)

9. GDP per capita affects and is affected by health conditions. While this two-way causality will be addressed later by correlating only initial health conditions with subsequent economic growth, reverse causality is also a statistical issue for the regressions in table 1.6. The effect of health on income can be addressed with an instrumental variables regression using openness of the economy as an instrument for GDP levels, as in Pritchett and Summers (1996). Openness is strongly correlated with GDP levels, but is unlikely to affect health conditions directly. There are no important changes to the coefficients after instrumenting (results not shown).

10. The OFDA/CRED International Disaster Database for 1900–1999 lists natural hazards that have caused 10 or more fatalities, affected 100 or more people, or resulted in a call for international assistance or the declaration of a state of emergency. The category for epidemics was excluded (CRED 2000).

11. Calculations based on Office of Foreign Disaster Assistance (1999) and Economic Commission for Latin America and the Caribbean (2000, p. 8).

12. Every 3 to 12 years, El Niño produces changes in the atmospheric circulation over the Pacific, thereby bringing about modified water temperatures off South America as well as floods and droughts on the Pacific slope of the continent.

13. According to Munich Reinsurance Group (1999), the number of major natural disasters between the 1960s and 1990s rose by a factor of three, with economic losses multiplied by nine. In 1998, more natural disasters occurred worldwide than in any other year on record. Note, however, that these comparisons may be affected to some degree by more accurate and comprehensive reporting of natural disasters in recent years.

14. The ratio of transport costs to local value added is equal to the costs of shipping the input in and the export out, all divided by the value of the output less the value of the imported inputs. For an export with a value of 1, imported inputs of 0.7 and shipping costs of 10 percent, that ratio is 56 percent

([0.1 × 0.7 + 0.1 × 1.0]/0.3). If shipping costs are only 5 percent, then the landed price of inputs is 5 percent less, or $0.7(1 - 0.05) = 0.665$, and value added is $1 - 0.665 = 0.335$. The ratio of shipping cost to value added is $0.05(1.665)/0.335 = 25$ percent.

15. Shipping cost data are hard to come by, but a recent study by the United Nations Conference on Trade and Development (UNCTAD) showed that for landlocked African countries, the cost of shipping a sea crate overland could be up to 228 percent of the cost of shipping the crate by sea from the nearest port to Europe; see Radelet and Sachs (1998).

16. Ades and Glaeser (1995) use a cross-section of 85 countries to study the effects of political and economic variables on *levels* of urban concentration. Gaviria and Stein (1999) use a panel of 105 countries and five decades to study the effects of a similar set of variables on *changes* in urban concentration.

17. See Glaeser (1998) for a complete analysis of the many agglomeration forces that affect productivity in cities.

18. More detailed descriptions of these variables can be found in Gallup, Sachs, and Mellinger (1999).

19. Notice that we lack a synthetic indicator for one of our channels of influence of geography, namely, propensity to natural disasters. However, in one of the regressions reported in table 1.9, we use as a rough indicator the reported rates of mortality caused by earthquakes and volcanic eruptions between 1902 and 1996, which is computed from data compiled by Office of Foreign Disaster Assistance (1999).

20. The dates are determined by data availability. The specifics of the variables used are found in Gallup, Sachs, and Mellinger (1999).

21. The results could suggest that, eventually, tropical countries with income levels beyond a certain threshold may grow even faster. However, the number of observations beyond that threshold is too small to warrant that conclusion.

22. See Tanzi and Davoodi (1997) for an analysis of the deleterious effects of corruption on the quality of infrastructure investments.

2

The Other Side of the Mountain: The Influence of Geography within Countries

THIS CHAPTER REEXAMINES THE connection between geography and economic development using a finer level of analysis.[1] Whereas the previous chapter showed that geographical conditions might account for a sizable portion of the differences in development *between* countries and regions of the world, this chapter attempts to trace the influence of geography *within* countries. Data for provinces and states of five Latin American countries show the complex channels through which climate, location, and other geographical features affect productivity, economic growth, health, and other development outcomes.

Chapter 1 uncovered various empirical associations between geography and development. Although these associations are rather suggestive, they do not always entail a causal link. Indeed, it can be argued that the connection between geography and development is ultimately driven by unobserved institutional factors that, for historical and other reasons, are correlated with geographical conditions. The important point here is that country studies in general—and the ones presented here in particular—are less subject to this type of criticism, if only because many formal institutions and cultural practices vary much less among regions within a country than among countries.

Country studies offer two additional advantages. First, they usually allow for more careful identification of the distinct pathways through which geography affects development. And second, they allow for the combination of statistical data with more detailed historical and ethnographical evidence. All in all, country studies provide an excellent complement to the more general (and hence more vague) cross-country evidence presented in the previous chapter.

It is also important to note that because people can usually move much more freely within national boundaries than across borders, country studies provide a litmus test for the presence of geographical effects. Indeed, if migration attenuates the effects of geography, as one would expect given people's tendency to escape adverse conditions, the effects of geography should be much smaller within countries. Therefore, if one finds that geographical forces do play a role within countries, this suggests that the same forces will play an even greater role in the larger context of countries and regions of the world.

This chapter focuses on five Latin American countries: Bolivia, Brazil, Colombia, Mexico, and Peru. The choice of countries is by no means arbitrary. All share two characteristics that make them excellent natural laboratories to study the connections between geographical conditions and economic development. First, they exhibit huge regional inequalities, and second, they are among the most geographically diverse countries of the world. The challenge is to establish the extent to which differences in living conditions between regions in these countries are driven by differences in geographical conditions.

A different set of issues is examined for each country. In this sense, the chapter resembles a loose travelogue in which the traveler focuses on a different aspect of each country without thinking too much about how the different pieces would fit together. Had we chosen to focus on the same set of issues in each country, we would have been able to draw more careful comparisons, but this would have come at the expense of losing the diversity of focus and methodology that gives this chapter much of its appeal.

We start our trip in Mexico, where we focus on the extent of regional inequalities and on the role of geographical conditions in the emergence and persistence of these inequalities. We show that geography can explain a substantial part of regional inequalities in both socioeconomic outcomes and political institutions. In Bolivia, we focus on the dynamics of regional development, with a particular emphasis on uncovering the geographical and economic factors underlying the growing prominence of the area in and around the city of Santa Cruz. From Bolivia we go to Colombia, where we also focus on issues of regional development. The emphasis is on studying the reasons why economic activity in Colombia has become increasingly concentrated around main urban centers, particularly Bogota. We finish our excursion around the Andean countries in Peru, where we study whether differences in geographical conditions between provinces can explain the corresponding differences in welfare and health conditions. The last leg of our trip takes us to Brazil, where we study the effects of climatic conditions on the prevalence of respiratory, water-borne, and vector-transmitted diseases.

Mexico

A mostly tropical country characterized by diverse geographical conditions, Mexico can be divided into three major geographical areas: the tropical coastal regions, the dry and warm north, and the relatively temperate central highlands.[2] A unique feature of the Mexican geography is its long border with the United States. Historically, trade and population flows have been dominated by the presence of the rich neighbor to the north.

Mexico's rugged geography includes both mountain chains of variable range and extended coastal areas. The presence of mountains and coasts plays a pervasive role in the determination of local climate conditions. Roughly speaking, dry areas constitute 40 percent of the national territory, tropical areas 20 percent, and temperate areas the remaining 40 percent.

Just as the climate conditions change substantially across the country, living conditions change dramatically from one Mexican state to another. The income per capita of the richest Mexican state (the Federal District) is more than five times greater than that of the poorest state (Oaxaca). Similar differences are found in illiteracy rates and the provision of public services. The female illiteracy rate is well above 30 percent in Chiapas and below 5 percent in the Federal District and Nuevo León. Similarly, in Oaxaca less than half of the households have access to sewerage, while in the Federal District almost all households are connected to some type of sewage system.

Map 2.1 (p. 99) shows the Mexican states and the differences in per capita income across them. Richer states are located to the north, with two exceptions, the Federal District and Campeche. The first houses the government and is the financial and business center of the country, while the second is home to much of the nation's oil production. Northern states, for their part, account for a significant amount of the country's industrial and agricultural production.

Geography and Institutions

While geography may help explain regional differences in Mexico, its effect is not direct and goes well beyond regional inequalities. Institutions are probably the most important channel through which geography influences regional patterns of development. Geography set the initial conditions for institutional development in the country, and these conditions have been perpetuated as a result of the path-dependent character of institutional change. That is, institutions have been an important pathway through which some initial characteristics of the landscape (many of them long forgotten) still affect economic development in Mexico.

Consider the following examples. Scholars from different disciplines have long studied the institutional arrangements of the pre-Hispanic societies of the central region of Mexico (Harris 1987; Palerm 1952; Wittofogel 1981). While their methodologies differ, they all consider the concept of "hydraulic societies." That is, the existence of numerous lakes in the central valleys of the Mexican high plateau created the need to control the occasional devastating floods and to store those same waters for irrigation. These needs in turn initiated a process of institution building that produced the types of societies the Spaniards found when they reached Mexico in the 16th century.

The Aztecs, Mayans, Mixtecs, Zapotecs, and Tarascans were all despotic societies in which heavy bureaucratic structures were supported by a large mass of landless peasants working small, communally held plots. These societies developed into centralized pre-states that depended on the tribute of many conquered peoples. Though these societies were technologically primitive in some respects, their social institutions were quite complex. Great cities and large populations attest to the efficacy of these institutional complexes. The Spanish conquistadors were able to adapt many of the existing indigenous institutions to their own purposes, as were the politicians who came to power after the Mexican Revolution in 1910. For example, the *ejido,* the most common form of land tenure in modern Mexico and a product of the revolution, is the direct descendant of the marriage of the medieval Spanish *ejido,* common land assigned to the townships, and the pre-Hispanic *calpulli,* state-held property worked by individual families. The regions where these "semi-hydraulic" pre-Hispanic civilizations were established—the Yucatan peninsula, the central valleys of Mexico, Michoacán, and Oaxaca—remain to this day areas where the "institutional density," as shown by the number of municipalities, is above the national average. In these regions it is still possible to observe some of the archaic institutions, including the *ejido,* adapted or not to the present conditions of modern Mexico.

This communal form of land tenure has maintained its central purpose for more than 700 years, namely, to control Mexico's many peasant communities. Control of these populations was originally needed to build and maintain the water works demanded by pre-Hispanic societies and colonial Mexico to survive. But when geography changed (lakes were eventually drained and the *chinampas*—man-made lake islands—became nothing more than a tourist attraction), the old institutions remained and their original purpose was redirected to serve new needs.

The *Partido Revolucionario Institucional* (PRI), the party established by the "revolutionary family" in the late 1920s, successfully used the *ejido* to keep political control of the country for more than 70 years. Discretionary land distribution among poor peasants and the subsequent creation of new *ejidos* tied the growing Mexican rural population to specific regions and transformed them into clients of the local political bosses. By contrast, the *ejido* was never used in the more sparsely populated areas of northern Mexico. The main priority there has never been to tie people to the land, but rather to cope with the poor natural conditions of the landscape. As a result, local institutions in northern Mexico have been more modern and amenable to adopting new technologies and exploring new sources of wealth. This difference in institutions may have a lot to do with the persistence of regional inequalities in Mexico. In sum, the current land tenure system in the poorest Mexican states (the same that allowed the PRI to maintain its power) can be traced back to the social organization of pre-Hispanic societies, which in turn can be traced back to the geographical conditions of pre-Hispanic Mexico.[3]

Another example of geography and development producing important institutional changes can be found in the Bajío region of north central Mexico during the early 19th century. The region is a fertile valley traversed by the Lerma River. The land is mostly flat and relatively close to the mining towns of Guanajuato, Querétaro, San Luis Potosí, Zacatecas, and Pachuca. Its population grew rapidly and developed modern agriculture to feed the surrounding booming silver mining towns. By the end of the 18th century, the Bajío was the breadbasket of Mexico. Thus, there were two very different economies symbiotically united in that relatively small area. On the one hand, the mining town economies were sustained by the exploitation of silver and subject to the rentier state. On the other, there was a modern agriculture sector composed of large private *haciendas* and small independent ranchers who were producing agricultural value through their hard work and improved technologies. These ranchers were subject to a more limited and modern institutional environment.

The Bajío's independent agricultural producers depended on the continuous flow of working capital provided by the Catholic Church, a large rentier with excess liquidity that provided many financial services to society at moderate rates. The Church as a financial institution had a long-term horizon. Its credits to the Bajío farmers were renewed routinely. However, in the early 1800s the King of Spain ordered the Mexican Church to provide him with a "forced" loan to pay for the European wars in which he was engaged. The Church began to call back its loans. The Bajío was suddenly plunged into a liquidity crisis. The tens of thousands of modern agricultural producers were suddenly stripped of vital financing. Discontent was widespread throughout the Bajío, and many Church leaders sympathized with the farmers. A potent revolutionary brew began to boil. Thus, the war of independence had found a fertile ground in the Bajío, the crossroads of two different economies, the rentier economy and the modern limited economy. Those individuals used to working under a modern limited institutional ecology would not readily accept the heavy-handedness of the rentier state structure. This conflict between a rentier heavy-handed state and social and economic agents developing in a more modern limited institutional ecology has been a constant throughout Mexico's modern history.

Geography and Development

Even at a first glance a strong connection between geography and development in Mexico is still evident today. The dry northern states are much richer than the southern tropical ones. Economic activity is sparse along the coast and intense in the center of the country. And natural resources are concentrated heavily in the southeast. These trends can be confirmed with statistical methods. Specifically, state-level data allow one to examine the association between GDP per capita (as measured in 1995) and four different groups of geographical variables: location, elevation, temperature, and rainfall. Each association should be examined separately to avoid problems stemming from the high correlation of the different geographical indicators.[4] Needless to say, the goal of this exercise is more descriptive than analytical, since these simple associations cannot capture the complex channels of influence of geography on development mentioned above.

The main results are shown in table 2.1. The first column shows that latitude is positively associated with income per capita: an increase of one degree (a little more than 100 kilometers) is associated with an increase of income per capita of almost 9 percent. Income per capita also increases as one moves from west to east: an increase of one degree in this direction is associated with an increase of 2.5 percent in GDP per capita.

The second column shows that, contrary to the international evidence presented in chapter 1, coastal states in Mexico are poorer

Table 2.1 Mexico: Geographical Variables and Income per Capita

Independent variable	Dependent variable: log of income per capita, 1995					
	[1]	[2]	[3]	[4]	[5]	[6]
Geographical position						
Latitude	0.087** (−3.96)					
Longitude	−0.025 (−1.47)					
Boundary[a]						
Coast		−0.078 (−0.55)				
U.S. border		0.515** (5.15)				
Log of altitude			−0.074* (−1.95)			
Climate[b]						
Humid				0.005 (1.67)		
Subhumid				0.011** (3.67)		
Semidry				0.012** (4.00)		
Very dry				0.014** (7.00)		
Cold				0.052** (5.20)		
Temperature					0.006** (0.23)	
Precipitation						−0.00033 (−2.54)
R^2	0.283	0.222	0.11	0.502	0.002	0.123
Observations	32	32	32	32	32	32

Notes: All regressions include a constant. t statistics are in parentheses.

a. Dummies by state (because the omitted variable is landlocked; the coefficients measure how much richer coastal or U.S border states are with respect to landlocked states).

b. Dummies by state (in this group of variables the omitted variable is temperate, with a similar interpretation).

*Significant at 10%.

**Significant at 5%.

Source: Esquivel (2000).

than landlocked ones. On the other hand, those states that share a border with the United States are, on average, 50 percent richer than the
rest of the states in the Mexican federation. These results should not
be surprising, since border states in Mexico play the role of coastal
states in other countries. They are home to the export industry and the
points of entry and exit for flows of commerce with the world's largest
market.

The third column shows that elevation is negatively associated with
GDP per capita. However, this association is weak and vanishes when
education is controlled for (Esquivel 2000). Ecological differences are
strongly associated with income levels, as shown in the fourth column.
Cold regions, which include the Federal District, are the richest, while
humid ones are the poorest. The fifth and sixth columns show that
temperature and rainfall are clearly associated with GDP per capita.
Blum and Díaz Cayeros (2002) show, however, that GDP per capita
and rainfall have a noticeable quadratic association: states with very
low or very high levels of rainfall tend to be richer than average,
whereas states with intermediate levels of rainfall (those around the
1,000-millimeter range) are the poorest.[5]

Judging by the statistical results, ecological features and proximity
to the United States are the strongest predictors of GDP per capita in
Mexico. However, states whose capitals are located at lower elevations and those that are located away from the coast, also tend to have
higher levels of development.

Convergence among States

Two main conclusions emerge from the discussion of the extent of regional inequalities in Mexico. First, regional inequalities are quite high
and, second, they are associated with a few geographical variables in
predictable ways. However, regional inequalities are an evolving trait
of Mexico's development pattern, as is the influence of geography.

Figure 2.1 measures the evolution of regional inequality in Mexico
from 1940 to 1995 using the standard deviation of state-level per
capita GDP (see Esquivel 1999 for a thorough description of the data).
Regional inequality fell sharply from 1940 to 1960, and since then it
has remained stable. These results are the same regardless of whether
they include the oil-producing states of Campeche and Tabasco.

Convergence rates provide an alternative way to look at the evolution of regional inequality.[6] Table 2.2 shows the rates of convergence
among Mexican states for three different periods: 1940–95, 1940–60,
and 1960–95. Convergence rates were very high in the first period but
fell substantially afterwards. Over the whole period, the rate of con-

Figure 2.1 Mexico: Income Disparities among States
(standard deviation of state level log per capita income)

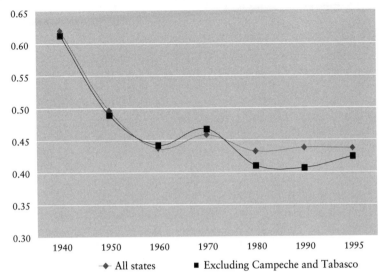

Source: Esquivel (2000).

vergence among Mexican states was well below the international standard of 2 percent a year (Barro and Sala-i-Martin 1992), which indicates that regional inequalities in Mexico have been very persistent when compared to international levels.

To shed some light on the source of this persistence, Esquivel (2000) examines the variation through time of the ranking of Mexican

Table 2.2 Rates of Convergence among Mexican States, 1940–95

Dependent variable: rate of annual average growth of state income per capita

Regression	Period	Rate of convergence	R^2
[1]	1940–95	0.012** (4.00)	0.507
[2]	1940–60	0.032** (3.94)	0.505
[3]	1960–95	0.009* (1.85)	0.134

Notes: All regressions include a constant. The rate of convergence is the coefficient at the beginning of the period of the state income level (in logs), which is the only independent variable in the regression; t statistics are in parentheses.
   *Significant at 10%.
   **Significant at 5%.
Source: Esquivel (2000).

states from 1940 to 1995. He shows that while there has been considerable churning among top and middle-income states, the states at the bottom of the ranking have always been the same. Indeed, four of the five poorest states in 1940—Chiapas, Guerrero, Michoacán, and Oaxaca—were also among the five poorest in 1995, which clearly suggests that persistent regional inequalities in Mexico may have a lot to do with the relative stagnation of the poorest Mexican states.

Can geographical conditions explain the persistence of regional inequalities in Mexico? Table 2.3 provides a preliminary answer to this question. This table shows the results of adding a few geographical indicators to the previous specification. There is a noticeable association between vegetation and economic growth: states where the vegetation is composed primarily of agricultural areas and woodlands tend to grow at lower rates. More important, convergence rates are somewhat higher once geographical conditions are controlled for, which suggests that geography may have slowed down the process of convergence among Mexican states. Indeed, one can argue that were Mexico a completely homogeneous country from a geographical standpoint, regional inequality would be at least 20 percent lower than what it is today.

But Mexico is not a homogeneous country geographically, and that has played an important role in its development from pre-Hispanic times to the present. The institutions born of geographical necessity centuries ago continue to exert influence over social and political life. Economically, elevation, temperature, rainfall, and vegetation have been and continue to be associated with important regional inequalities in growth and development.

Bolivia

Bolivia's wide-ranging geography includes high mountains in the west, mild valleys in the central region, and hot and humid lowlands in the east.[7] Bolivia has traditionally been divided into three geological regions: the Andean or mountainous region, the sub-Andean or valley region, and the lowland region (see map 2.2, p. 100). Although this division entails considerable simplification, it will be used here because it is standard in much of the local literature, and because much of the necessary data is divided along those lines.

The socioeconomic divisions of Bolivia do not perfectly overlap with the geographical regions described above. As shown in map 2.3 (p. 100), Bolivia has nine departments and more than 100 provinces. Unfortunately, most of the relevant data are available only at the depart-

Table 2.3 Geography and Convergence among Mexican States

Independent variable	Dependent variable: rate of income growth per state capita, 1940–95						
	[1]	[2]	[3]	[4]	[5]	[6]	[7]
Log of income per capita, 1940	-0.014**	-0.014**	-0.014**	-0.015**	-0.015**	-0.015**	-0.015**
	(-6.02)	(-6.13)	(-6.33)	(-6.44)	(-6.46)	(-6.20)	(-5.37)
Humid climate (% of state area)	-0.008*	-0.007	-0.006	-0.005	-0.005	-0.007	-0.005
	(-1.81)	(-1.54)	(-1.34)	(-1.17)	(-1.09)	(-1.53)	(-1.23)
Cold climate (% of state area)	0.040**	0.040**	0.025*	0.026*	0.025*	0.021	0.025*
	(3.96)	(3.83)	(1.86)	(1.82)	(1.81)	(1.44)	(1.81)
Woodland (% of state area)	-0.024**	-0.024**	-0.018**	-0.018**	-0.018*	-0.015**	-0.018*
	(-2.55)	(-2.37)	(-2.16)	(-2.04)	(-1.99)	(-2.11)	(-1.89)
Agricultural vegetation (% of state area)	-0.015**	-0.015**	-0.014**	-0.014**	-0.00013**	-0.013**	-0.013**
	(-3.21)	(-2.94)	(-3.34)	(-3.07)	(-2.76)	(-3.59)	(-2.87)
Log of minimal distance to some border city in the United States		-0.001		-0.001			
		(-0.45)		(-0.36)			
Urban population, 1940 (% of state population)			0.011	0.010	0.011*	0.000	0.000
			(1.69)	(1.51)	(1.73)	(1.10)	(1.34)

(Table continues on the following page.)

Table 2.3 (continued)

Independent variable				*Dependent variable: rate of income growth per state capita, 1940–95*			
	[1]	[2]	[3]	[4]	[5]	[6]	[7]
Latitude					0.006 (0.21)		
Access to potable water 1940 (% of housing in state)						0.009 (0.82)	
Rate of illiteracy, 1940 (% of the population > 15 years old)							−0.002 (−0.13)
R^2 adjusted	0.733	0.736	0.752	0.754	0.753	0.762	0.753
Observations	32	32	32	32	32	32	32
F statistic	14.266	11.604	12.650	10.523	10.439	10.963	10.426

Notes: All regressions include a constant. The standard errors are corrected by heteroelasticity according to White's method; t statistics are in parentheses.
*Significant at 10%.
**Significant at 5%.
Source: Esquivel (2000).

mental level, meaning that some correspondence between departments and regions must be established. Following a standard practice in the local literature, this section assumes that the Andean region comprises the departments of La Paz, Oruro, and Potosí; the sub-Andean region the departments of Chuquisaca, Cochabamba, and Tarija; and the lowland region the departments of Beni, Pando, and Santa Cruz.

Table 2.4 displays some basic geographical features of Bolivia's three regions. The Andean region is located at a mean altitude of roughly 3,700 meters (about 12,000 feet) above sea level. Its proximity to the equator notwithstanding, the Andean region contains areas with decidedly nontropical climates. At higher elevations, for instance, snowfall is common. At the other extreme, the mean altitude of the lowland region is close to sea level, and temperatures are what would be expected given its tropical location. The sub-Andean region has intermediate levels of elevation and temperature and is by far the smallest of the three regions.

Table 2.4 Description of Bolivia's Three Geographical Regions

Indicator	Andean	Sub-Andean	Lowlands
Mean altitude[a]	3,770 m	2,405 m	267 m
	(12,361 ft.)	(7,885 ft.)	(875 ft.)
Mean altitude[b]	3,970 m	2,150 m	291 m
	(13,016 ft.)	(7,049 ft.)	(954 ft.)
Mean temperature (Celsius)[a]	15.0	21.8	27.3
Mean temperature (Fahrenheit)[a]	59.0	71.2	81.1
Maximum temperature (Celsius)[c]	19.2	34.9	35.8
Minimum temperature (Celsius)[c]	−4.7	6.6	13.4
Total area (percent)[c]	28	13	59
Total forested lands (percent)[c]	11	13	77
Total permanent snow and ice-covered areas (percent)[c]	100	0	0
Total humid areas (percent)[c]	1	2	97

a. Derived from city level data (departmental capitals).
b. Derived from departmental data.
c. Based on data provided by the Geographic Military Institute.
Source: Urquiola and others (2000), based on publications and data from the National Statistics Institute and the National Geographic Military Institute.

Table 2.5 Bolivia: Regional Patterns of Production, Disease, and Language
(percent)

Indicator	Andean	Sub-Andean	Lowlands
Total population in 1992	45.0	28.9	26.1
Production share			
Rice production, total			
1994–95 crop	6.0	5.8	88.2
Potato production, total			
1994–95 crop	48.7	42.8	8.4
Coffee production, total			
1994–95 crop	96.4	1.1	2.5
Grape production, total			
1994–95 crop	23.9	73.2	2.9
Tomato production, total			
1994–95 crop	5.7	6.6	87.7
Disease prevalence			
Cholera and malaria, total			
1995 cases	7.1	41.0	51.9
Language			
Aymara	39.7	3.7	2.0
Quechua	24.8	49.9	11.2

Note: All information derived from departmental data.

Source: Urquiola and others (1999), based on Instituto Nacional de Estadística (1997a, 1997b).

In Bolivia, geographical differences have produced stark interregional differences in patterns of agricultural production. Table 2.5 shows that more than 90 percent of potato production takes place in the Andean or sub-Andean regions, while a similar percentage of rice production takes place in the lowlands. The production of coffee, grapes, and tomatoes shows similarly skewed regional distributions. Table 2.5 also shows that the incidence of tropical diseases varies considerably between regions. The Andean region, home to 45 percent of the population, accounts for only 7 percent of all cholera and malaria cases, while the lowlands region accounts for 52 percent of cases with only 26 percent of the population.

Geographical differences may partially explain why different pre-Columbian civilizations came to dominate each geographical region. Stark differences in climate and soil conditions may have laid the foundation for the emergence of specific cultures, each circumscribed to a particular region. Although these civilizations are presumed to have traded extensively among one another, they never completely intermingled. One present day vestige of this historical phenomenon is the prevalence of native languages within each region, also shown in table 2.5. Aymara is the most common native language in the Andean region, while Quechua, the language of the Incas, has greater influence in the sub-Andean region. The lowlands region has a noticeable share of Guaraní speakers (not shown in the table), a native language more common in areas of Paraguay and Brazil.

Geography and Regions

Historically, the population of Bolivia has been disproportionately concentrated in the Andean region, followed by the sub-Andean and lowland regions. Figure 2.2 shows, however, that, at least since the 1950s, the lowlands region has been steadily gaining importance at the expense of the Andean region.[8] Differences in migration patterns rather than in fertility rates underlie the growing importance of the lowlands. Table 2.6 shows that whereas all three Andean departments had negative net migration rates during 1987–92, all lowland departments had positive migration rates. Santa Cruz deserves special mention, as it had a net migration rate close to 20 percent.

As in most developing countries, urbanization in Bolivia increased steadily during the period under study. In 1950, no region of the country had an urbanization rate above 30 percent. Forty years later, the rate of urbanization was higher than 50 percent in the country as a whole and as high as 70 percent in the lowlands. Yet unlike many developing countries, Bolivia has not urbanized around a single clearly

Figure 2.2 Bolivia: Population Distribution by Region

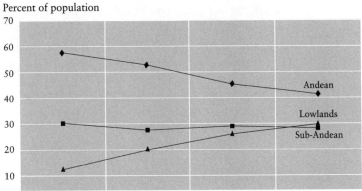

Source: Urquiola and others (1999).

Table 2.6 Bolivia: Net Migration and Population Growth
Rates, by Department, 1971–92

Region	Department	Net migration[a] 1971–76	Net migration[a] 1987–92	1976–92 total population growth (%)
Andean	La Paz	1.4	−1.4	16.6
	Oruro	2.4	−12.5	5.8
	Potosí	−3.1	−12.4	−1.2
Sub-Andean	Chuquisaca	−4.7	−3.7	15.0
	Cochabamba	3.1	4.7	27.5
	Tarija	10.6	6.4	28.2
Lowlands	Beni	−2.1	0.6	31.6
	Pando	14.1	2.3	6.3
	Santa Cruz	6.7	19.0	41.6

a. Net migration rate per 1,000 persons per year.
Source: Urquiola and others (1999) based on Instituto Nacional de Estadística
(1997a).

dominant city. Figure 2.3 shows that the percentage of the urban population living in La Paz, the largest city of the country, has declined
from almost 40 percent in 1950 to barely 29 percent in 2001. However, the decline of urban concentration in the country as a whole has
been accompanied by the rising dominance of one city within each of
the three regions: La Paz in the Andean region, Cochabamba in the
sub-Andean region, and Santa Cruz in the lowlands.

These three cities form the central axis of the country. La Paz is an
important transit location toward the Pacific Ocean, while Santa Cruz,
located at the other extreme of the axis, is important for transit toward
Brazil. Data from the 1996 round of the National Employment Survey
(ENE) show that 53 percent of the Bolivian population lives within
two hours by car of the central axis. Population density declines
steadily as one moves away from the axis, to the point where provinces
located 15 or more hours by car from the central axis have a population density below one inhabitant per square kilometer.

Why has the urban population in Bolivia concentrated around these
well-defined centers? Geography may have a lot to do with it. The
presence of well-defined geographical regions that closely overlap with
the main linguistic divisions of the country may have prevented many
city-bound migrants from straying far from their regions. Put simply,
lowlanders are reluctant to move to La Paz and highlanders are reluctant to move to Santa Cruz. As a result, rural-urban migration has occurred disproportionately within regions, which in turn has given rise
to three main regional population centers.

Because altitude gives rise to Bolivia's geographical diversity, elevation differences have also contributed to relatively high transport
costs. Road construction is expensive in the Andean and sub-Andean
regions because of the highly mountainous topography. Soft soil and
abundant rain make the construction and particularly the maintenance
of reliable paved roads expensive in the lowlands as well. The combination of these factors determines that once roads are built, transport
costs are in fact lower in the Andean than in the lowland regions.
Overall, Bolivia has the lowest road density (kilometers per million inhabitants) of any South American country. Despite a large increase between the 1960s and 1990s, it still has the least amount of kilometers
of paved roads.

While geographical and ethnic differences are arguably the main
structural forces behind the spatial distribution of today's population
in Bolivia, they can hardly account for the growing importance of the
lowlands in general and of the city of Santa Cruz in particular. To understand the emergence of Santa Cruz, one needs to know what has
sustained its booming economy and what made it possible in the first
place.

Figure 2.3 Bolivia: Urban Primacy Indexes by Region

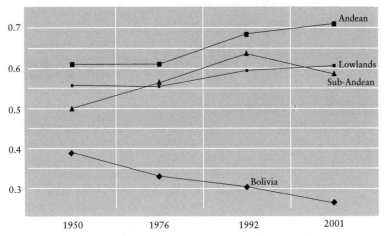

Note: Based on metropolitan area rather than city proper data. This distinction
matters mainly for La Paz, where the metropolitan area consists of two well-defined
cities, El Alto and La Paz. Because El Alto and La Paz are contiguous cities with
integrated labor markets, the use of metropolitan areas seems more appropriate in
this case.
Source: Urquiola and others (1999).

A substantial part of the recent economic growth of Santa Cruz has its origin in geographical factors. Activities related to the area's natural resources have been on the increase since 1950. A significant portion of them is related to relatively large-scale agricultural production favored by the fertile land in parts of this department. Interestingly, agricultural growth in Santa Cruz has not been driven by a single crop, but rather by a succession of crops that, each in its turn, has given the area several successive "booms." In chronological order, these crops have been rice, cotton, sugar cane, and soybeans.

Table 2.7 illustrates this point. The first column shows the 15-fold increase in the total area under cultivation in the department of Santa Cruz between 1950 and 1997. In contrast, the total area under cultivation in the Andean region has remained stagnant since 1950. The remaining columns of the table show the percentage of the total area accounted for by particular crops. The highlighted cell in each column corresponds to the period when the crop in question reached its highest share in the total cultivated area. As shown, each of these products has at some point dominated agricultural production in Santa Cruz, yet none except for soybeans has held such a position for more than a few years.

Beyond these agricultural booms, Santa Cruz has also experienced an oil- and especially gas-related boom, despite the fact that a substantial part of the oil industry is actually located in two other departments, Tarija and Cochabamba. Santa Cruz has also benefited from the relocation of the industry's headquarters to its capital city.

Table 2.7 Bolivia: Crop Shares in the Total Area under Cultivation, Santa Cruz

Period	Total area under cultivation (hectares)	Rice	Cotton	Sugar cane	Soybean	Other
1950	58,242	17.4	0.2	18.1	0.0	64.3
1958	125,000	10.8	0.6	12.0	0.0	76.6
1964	154,370	16.1	2.3	16.4	0.0	65.3
1969–71	173,612	22.8	6.8	17.3	0.5	52.6
1971–75	217,618	16.8	22.5	17.7	1.9	41.0
1975–80	258,332	13.3	12.2	23.8	7.6	43.1
1980–84	263,464	15.9	3.6	21.0	13.5	46.0
1990–94	573,058	14.7	3.2	11.6	39.6	30.9
1994–97	945,244	9.1	4.3	7.7	48.8	30.0

Note: The highlighted cells mark the crop's highest share over the period.
Source: Urquiola and others (1999) based on Arrieta (1994) and UDAPE (1998).

While activities related to Santa Cruz's natural resources have enjoyed significant growth since 1950, those based upon the natural resource endowments of the Andean region have been in steep decline. The prime example of this has been the contraction in mining. Indeed, this is reflected in the relative decline of Potosí and especially Oruro, the two traditional mining cities, in the country's urban rankings.

Of course, natural resource potential and migration may be necessary, but are not sufficient, conditions for the rapid growth by Santa Cruz. Additionally, capital from both the public and private sectors has helped propel the region's expansion. In the 1940s and 1950s, the national government, partially as a result of recommendations made by a commission led by Merwin Bohan, adopted a lowlands-oriented growth strategy. A new highway was built connecting Cochabamba to Santa Cruz, as were numerous minor roads connecting smaller towns within the lowlands. Generous incentives were granted to rice and sugar producers in Santa Cruz and to cattle ranchers in Beni. Lending from the state-owned agricultural bank was concentrated in and around Santa Cruz. In sum, Santa Cruz was a net recipient of government transfers for much of the period under study. Only in the mid-1990s did the situation change, with Santa Cruz contributing more than what it received in the way of public funds. Last, but not least, agricultural production around Santa Cruz benefited from closer integration between Bolivia and Brazil. As better roads helped reduce transportation costs and trade became less regulated and taxed, investment opportunities improved for both locals and outsiders.

Thus, the emergence of Santa Cruz can be traced to successive agricultural booms that, at least in the initial stages, were facilitated by the deliberate efforts of the government to steer the development of Bolivia toward this area. The growing importance of Santa Cruz was not accompanied, however, by a concentration of industrial production in and around this city. Table 2.8 uses an index that ranges between zero and two, where zero indicates that regions are identical or lack any specialization, and two indicates completely specialized regions. The table shows that these coefficients are very low and have changed little, suggesting that the regions are hardly differentiated and have not become more specialized over time. That is, industrial production in Bolivia still has a predominantly local character that specializes in meeting the needs of its regions rather than in competing at a national level.

Geography and Welfare

While geographical factors have played a role in determining where people live, it is now interesting to consider geography's influence on

Table 2.8 Bolivia: Concentration Indexes by Geographical
Regions, 1976 and 1992

Region	Lowlands	Sub-Andean
1976		
Lowlands	—	0.2740
Andean	0.1901	0.2151
1992		
Lowlands	—	0.3430
Andean	0.2608	0.0958

— Not available.

Note: This table uses Krugman's regional specialization index. Applied to location pairs, this index is defined as $SI_{jk} = \Sigma_i \mid E_{ij}/E_j - E_{ik}/E_k \mid$, where E_{ij} is employment in industry i in region j, E_j is total employment in region j, and E_{ik} and E_k are the corresponding values for region k.

Source: Urquiola and others (1999).

the well-being of those people. The previous section showed how Bolivia's population is concentrated along a central axis defined by three regional capitals, which have varied considerably in their growth rates. This section looks at whether altitude and distance from regional centers are associated with the incidence of poverty in Bolivia.

In considering geography's impact on welfare, provinces are the relevant units of observation.[9] The dependent variable is based on the Unsatisfied Basic Needs (UBN) Index calculated by the Bolivian government using the 1976 and 1992 censuses.[10] To construct the dependent variable, the UBN index is first used to determine whether a household has satisfied its basic needs, and then this information is used to calculate the incidence of poverty in the province under analysis.

Table 2.9 shows the effects of geographical variables on provincial-level UBN poverty indices. When interpreting the results, it is important to keep in mind that higher UBN indices indicate higher poverty levels. The first column shows that provinces at higher elevations have a higher incidence of poverty, which is consistent with the Mexican evidence in the previous section. However, because of the inverse relation between mean altitude and temperature, this result is counter to the usual international evidence suggesting that tropical areas in fact have lower incomes. The second column shows that the relationship between poverty and altitude is not monotonic but quadratic; poverty levels are higher at both very low and very high altitudes.

Table 2.9 also shows that the incidence of poverty is lower in provinces that contain either a major border crossing or a department

capital or regional center. As in the case of Colombia, which will follow, distance from major domestic markets is a strong predictor of
poverty in Bolivia. Similarly, provinces where agriculture constitutes a
large portion of total production have higher poverty rates, all else being equal.[11]

In sum, in Bolivia the incidence of poverty is greater in provinces of
high elevation and in provinces located farther away from the
country's main commercial axis. Whether this reflects a direct effect of
geography on welfare or the concentration of poor households in high
elevation and remote provinces is still unresolved. Preliminary analy-
ses, however, based on household data, show that the effect of
geography is still apparent even after taking into account provincial
differences in household characteristics. Certainly, anyone who has
laid eyes on the barren Bolivian altiplano or negotiated the precipitous
roads to the steamy lowlands suspects that these stark geographical,
elements may have had an influence on the country's widespread
poverty. The job for academics is to more thoroughly analyze the
channels of that influence and to propose better ways to rein it in.

Table 2.9 Bolivia: Geographical Variables and Provincial-Level
Unsatisfied Basic Needs

Independent variable	Dependent variable = UBN index				
	[1]	[2]	[3]	[4]	[5]
Altitude	0.023**	−0.008	(−0.017)	−0.012	−0.032**
	(2.30)	(−0.21)	(−0.45)	(−0.38)	(−2.00)
Altitude		0.008	0.009	0.008	0.011**
squared		(0.89)	(1.00)	(1.00)	(0.01)
Border			−0.118**	−0.132**	−0.137**
crossing			(−2.41)	(−3.22)	(−6.52)
Regional				−0.422**	0.095**
center				(−6.59)	(−1.79)
Department					−0.135**
capital					(−4.66)
Agriculture					0.188**
(percent)					(9.90)
Density					−.009
					(−9.00)
R²	0.021	0.059	0.113	0.393	0.850
Observations	99	99	99	99	99

Note: All regressions include a constant term. t statistics are in parentheses.
**Significant at 5%.
Source: Urquiola and others (1999).

Colombia

Colombia is a country not only of great geographical differences, but of profound variations in economic and social development among and within regions.[12] Geography has had a substantial influence on its economic history, particularly with respect to the spatial distribution of economic activity among the country's widely disparate regions.

Until recently, economic activity in Colombia was divided into four well-defined zones: Tolima and Huila and the highest eastern plateaus, the Atlantic coastal region, Antioquia, and the Pacific coast departments. Economic activity within each zone was in turn organized around a single city: Bogota, Barranquilla, Medellín, and Cali, respectively (see map 2.4, p. 101). This demographic pattern led some authors to describe Colombia's urban development as a "four-headed beast" (Cuervo and González 1997; Gouesset 1998).

Regional fragmentation and the concomitant absence of a national market have long been common topics among observers of the Colombian economy. In 1950, Lauchlin Currie wrote:

> One extremely significant consequence of the topography of the country has been the emergence of four fairly distinct and separate economic entities or trading zones. Each of these zones includes lands and climates permitting a wide diversity of agricultural production. Each has a metropolitan area whose food requirements are met very largely within the zone. Within each zone the transport facilities permit considerable movement of agricultural commodities. This self-contained characteristic extends even in part to industry. Each of the zones supplies all or part of its own requirements for cement, most building materials, cotton textiles and beer. Curiously enough, each zone contains coal. The goods that move across zonal lines are those that can bear high transport costs; and comprise mainly salt, sugar, oil, imported and exported goods.

The country's geographical barriers, some of which were not overcome until very late in the 20th century, cut off many regions from world markets and discouraged interregional trade, giving rise to a fragmented domestic market. Even those roads and railroads built at the end of the 19th century were designed to connect towns and villages within the same region. In order for roads to connect different regions they would often need to traverse Colombia's mountainous areas, and construction costs were prohibitively high. As a result, Colombia's regions have experienced a high degree of geographical and economic isolation that in many respects persists to the present day as the country continues to have one of the lowest road densities in Latin America.

Since colonization, the population of Colombia has been concentrated in the mountainous west and north of the country. It was in these areas that, in the late 19th century, coffee production established itself as Colombia's main agricultural and export product and early manufacturing industries were born. From that time until the 1970s, most of the population lived in rural areas near small towns and villages whose primary sources of income were agriculture and livestock. This period also saw the growth of an urban population in the four main cities.

The urban centers within each zone consolidated their dominance late in the 19th century. The port city of Barranquilla had its golden age during that time and into the early 20th century. Commercial activities, prompted in part by foreign immigration, contributed greatly to the initial expansion of Barranquilla (Posada 1998). The central city of Medellín also grew very rapidly at the turn of the century. Initially a trading post for coffee growers and gold miners, Medellín would later emerge as a booming manufacturing center. The capital of Bogota, located in the eastern mountains, has historically been Colombia's cultural and political center. Lastly, the city of Cali, surrounded by the fertile Cauca Valley and initially the home of rich *hacendados,* would later become a booming agricultural and depot center.

Although geography has been neglected in regional and municipal economic growth models and estimations in Colombia, historians and travelers have long noted the important role of geographical factors in Colombian development. John Hamilton, a British colonel traveling in Colombia in the 19th century, highlighted in 1829 the heavy burden that nature and climate imposed on trade and human transportation. The trip down the Magdalena River from Barranquilla to Honda, the only access to Bogota, lasted more than 100 days. During such a long journey, many passengers fell ill or died of malaria, yellow fever, diarrhea, and cholera. High freight costs, moreover, made trade expensive, impeding the import of goods and machinery to the hinterland (Hamilton 1970).

James Parsons, a sociologist who studied in depth the colonization of Antioquia, suggested that the longstanding isolation of mountainous inner Colombia had defined the traditionalism, and peculiar cultural features, of the Antioquians (Parsons 1997). The scarcity of an indigenous labor force and the near nonexistence of flatlands meant that, by the 19th century, the rural population of Antioquia was composed mainly of small landholders. This prompted the early democratic tradition of the Antioquian labor force, in contrast with the classist social structure found in the south and west of Colombia, where there was a higher indigenous population. The special characteristics of this society, the result of geographical features, determined in part the early industrialization of the region.

The geography of the Caribbean coast likewise brought about a distinctive pattern of development. The sea, rivers, and swamps determined the position of the main settlements on the coast in terms of access to and sources of water and food. Life was not easy: land and towns suffered periodic floods that destroyed houses and crops and altered the geography of the region. Floods and high temperatures encouraged the proliferation of diseases, infections, and plagues, and made the establishment of long-term mining or manufacturing activities difficult.

The lack of economic opportunities and the high level of disease on the coast resulted in migration, death, and slow population growth, which generated labor scarcity. The latter, along with low productivity of labor, outdated technology, and poor transport, hampered the rise of commercial plantations (*haciendas*), limiting the development of agriculture until very late in the 20th century. In contrast, the region's land characteristics and market conditions facilitated the rise and consolidation of cattle-raising.

Leading historians, economists, and sociologists have recognized the crucial role of geography in shaping regional development patterns in Colombia. The main factors by which geography has directly conditioned economic development are transport costs, health factors, and natural resources (land suitability, water, closeness to rivers, and so on). If these factors influence population density and creation of markets, they also have indirect effects on growth dynamics through agglomeration economies and other feedback mechanisms.

Geography and Municipal Growth

Although geography played a pivotal role in the initial distribution of economic activity in Colombia, its current role is an open question. This section examines the determinants of municipal growth in Colombia, with a special emphasis on the role of geographical indicators. The analysis focuses on explaining the growth of municipal GDP per capita between 1973 and 1995.[13] The influence of geography is captured by the inclusion of such variables as soil quality, water availability, and distance to the country's main urban centers. In addition to geographical indicators, explanatory variables include human capital, infrastructure, and institutional variables. This provides a means of checking whether the influence of geography is still present in a direct way (rather than indirectly through the endowments of physical, human, or social capital).

Table 2.10 shows that geography is related to municipal income growth in predictable ways.[14] Municipalities with more fertile soil, less rugged topography, and moderate weather conditions (for example, intermediate elevation) tend to grow faster. More rainfall is associated with slower growth, as is being closer to a large river.

Municipal growth in Colombia is also strongly associated with the distance from the country's main urban centers. Municipalities far from the main population centers have grown much more slowly. Thus, the growth of municipalities on the periphery, some of which were already in a precarious situation in 1973, has continued to dwindle, at least until 1995.

Needless to say, geographical variables are not the only factors that influence municipal growth. The estimates in the second column of table 2.10 consider the possible influence of physical infrastructure, human capital, and some other factors.[15] Not surprisingly, a wider coverage of basic infrastructure services, such as electricity, accelerates economic growth. A municipality where all households have access to electricity tends to grow 2 percentage points faster than another where no household has electricity. Similarly, all else being equal, municipalities with higher initial stocks of human capital tend to grow more rapidly. Both primary and secondary enrollment and the stock of college graduates (at the beginning of the period of analysis) are associated with higher levels of growth (during the period of analysis). One additional college graduate per 1,000 persons in 1973 is associated with 0.1 percentage point of additional annual growth subsequently. Of course, this may reflect not so much the benefits of higher education as the desire of college graduates to locate in areas with high growth prospects.

The incidence of tropical diseases also seems to have hampered municipal growth. Interestingly, this effect holds up even after controlling for some geographical variables associated with the incidence of tropical diseases (such as rainfall and the effects of the Cauca and Magdalena Rivers).[16]

Surprisingly, coffee is negatively associated with municipal growth. All else being equal, the higher the proportion of land dedicated to coffee cultivation in a municipality, the slower its growth rate. This result flies in the face of the widespread belief that coffee and economic prosperity have moved hand in hand in Colombia. If anything, coffee has spelled stagnation in the country's recent history, due in part to the bleak international coffee market.

Table 2.10 Colombia: Determinants of Municipal per Capita
Income Growth, 1973–95

Independent variable	[1]	[2]
Per capita income, 1973	−0.022 (−14.73)**	−0.028 (−14.80)**
Geography		
Rain	−0.014 (−4.82)**	−0.009 (−3.58)**
Altitude above sea level	0.009 (1.89)*	0.011 (2.04)**
Altitude above sea level squared	−0.001 (−1.54)	−0.001 (−1.85)*
Soil suitability index	0.017 (4.98)**	0.013 (3.08)**
Distance to domestic markets	−0.057 (−14.17)**	−0.045 (−11.05)**
Cauca River (dummy)	−0.014 (−1.95)*	−0.012 (−1.72)*
Magdalena River (dummy)	−0.005 (−0.95)	−0.001 (−0.25)
River (distance to, in kilometers)	0.009 (3.66)**	0.005 (2.08)**
Infrastructure		
Proportion of households with electrical power, 1973		0.022 (2.77)**
Road density, 1970		0.0004 (0.59)
Human capital		
Migration rate, 1973		0.092 (5.78)**
Enrollment rate in primary and secondary school, 1973		0.081 (5.25)**
College graduates per thousand of labor force, 1973		0.001 (3.31)**
Number of tropical disease deaths per 1,000 people, 1973		−0.004 (−2.67)**
Institutions and living standards		
Interaction between soil and degree of urbanization, 1973		−0.003 (−1.20)
Proportion of land with coffee crops, 1980		−0.0004 (−3.93)**
Income inequality, 1973		−0.003 (−0.81)
R^2	0.35	0.486
Observations	873	872

Note: All regressions include a constant term. t statistics are in parentheses.
  *Significant at 10%.
  **Significant at 5%.
Source: Sánchez and Núñez (2000).

The results of table 2.10 are also consistent with the idea of conditional convergence, that is, the tendency of municipal income levels to move toward a common level once the influence of other determinants of those incomes is taken into account. All else being equal, higher levels of GDP per capita in 1973 are associated with slower growth. But *conditional* convergence does not necessarily mean that municipal inequality has declined in Colombia, because the host of variables that influence growth (other than initial income levels) may affect rich and poor municipalities differently. Indeed, the coefficient of variation of municipal per capita GDP increased from 0.61 in 1973 to 0.67 in 1995, suggesting a slight rise in inequality across municipalities.

Clearly, a number of factors ranging from human capital to access to electricity play a role in determining municipal growth. However, even when all these factors are controlled for, the influence of geography is confirmed. Therefore, geography is still affecting regional development patterns in a direct way, not just through the influence that it may have had on infrastructure, education, or institutional variables in the past. Surprisingly, investments in physical, human, or social capital have done little to compensate for (or to reinforce) the influence of geography in the speed of economic development of Colombian municipalities, as evidenced by comparing the coefficients of the two regressions in table 2.10.

Differences in Levels of Development across Municipalities

If geography has influenced and is still influencing municipal growth, current income levels would also be expected to show the heavy mark of geography. Table 2.11 analyzes the determinants of municipal GDP per capita in 1995 using a similar set of explanatory variables as before. The results confirm that geography has had a pervasive influence on the extremely diverse levels of development of Colombian municipalities.

Successful municipalities in Colombia tend to have "better" geography and cluster around the country's main urban centers. That is, on average, wealthier municipalities have less rainfall, better soils, and flatter topographies than poorer ones. Moreover, wealthier municipalities are located closer to Colombia's principal centers of development, but far away from the main rivers. The influence of each and all of these geographical factors on income levels is moderated but remains significant when infrastructure, human capital, and institutional factors come into play. This amounts to saying that geography does seem to have a direct impact on income levels, in addition to the indirect effect that it may have because of its influence on physical and

Table 2.11 Colombia: Determinants of Municipal per Capita Income Growth, 1995

Independent variable	[1]	[2]
Geography		
Rain	−0.589	−0.341
	(−8.16)**	(−5.69)**
Altitude above sea level	0.426	0.36
	(2.68)**	(2.78)**
Altitude above sea level squared	−0.039	−0.033
	(−2.73)**	(−2.80)**
Soil suitability index	0.672	0.482
	(8.155)**	(5.15)**
Distance to domestic markets	−1.497	−1.105
	(−12.72)**	(−10.37)**
Cauca River (dummy)	−0.508	−0.413
	(−2.21)**	(−2.68)**
Magdalena River (dummy)	−0.099	−0.034
	(−0.68)	(−0.27)
River (distance to, in kilometers)	0.267	0.171
	(3.94)**	(2.90)**
Infrastructure		
Proportion of households		0.817
with electrical power, 1973		(3.95)**
Road density, 1970		0.057
		(2.05)**
Rate of growth of road density		0.662
		(1.84)*
Human capital		
Migration rate, 1973		2.636
		(5.92)**
Enrollment rate in primary		1.981
and secondary school, 1973		(5.10)**
College graduates per thousand		0.037
of labor force, 1973		(2.85)**
Number of tropical disease deaths		−0.096
per thousand people, 1979		(−2.73)**
Institutions and living standards		
Interaction between soil and		−0.112
degree of urbanization, 1973		(−2.06)**

Independent variable	[1]	[2]
Proportion of land with		−0.012
coffee crops, 1980		(−4.52)**
Income inequality, 1973		0.007
		(0.09)
Per capita municipal transfers		0.44
(yearly average 1973–95)		(5.22)**
R^2	0.353	0.554
Observations	873	872

Note: All regressions include a constant term. t statistics are in parentheses.
*Significant at 10%.
**Significant at 5%.
Source: Sánchez and Núñez (2000).

human investment and a variety of other channels that can be measured across municipalities.

Interestingly, however, geographical variables seem to be more significant for poor municipalities than for rich ones. In poor municipalities, geography explains between 25 and 32 percent of income per capita variation and between 24 and 27 percent of income per capita growth variations.[17] In contrast, in rich municipalities, geography is less important, explaining between 18 and 25 percent of income per capita variation and between 16 and 17 percent of income per capita growth variation. What this suggests is encouraging: although the influence of geography is still present, economic and social development tends to loosen its tight dominance.

The Geography of Success for Colombian Municipalities

The fates of many municipalities in Colombia changed dramatically from 1973 to 1995: some doubled their income, while others experienced threefold declines. This was not just the result of chance. As already shown, proximity to major cities has been a powerful engine of municipal growth, and the explanation lies to a large extent on this factor. However, the influence of proximity has changed over time depending on transportation improvements and the evolving nature of development policies.

At the beginning of the 1980s, Bogota's economic growth and development left the rest of the principal Colombian cities behind. As Colombian economic activity moved toward Bogota in the 1980s, major changes in the spatial variation of average municipal per capita income resulted. Figure 2.4 shows this variation of per capita income growth as one moves from municipalities close to Bogota to those lo-

Figure 2.4 Colombia: Municipalities per Capita Income
Growth and Distance from Bogota

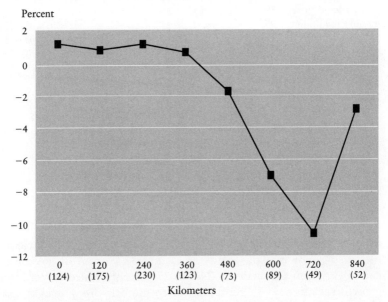

Percent

Note: Numbers in parentheses are sample sizes for each distance.
Source: Sánchez and Núñez (2000).

cated on the periphery of the country. The leftmost dot shows the average growth of municipal per capita income of Bogota. The next dot
shows the corresponding average growth for all municipalities located
within 120 kilometers of Bogota (excluding Bogota), the next dot
shows the corresponding average for all municipalities located within
240 kilometers of Bogota but outside the previous circles, and so on in
a sequence of concentric circles. Clearly, those municipalities located
far from Bogota fared much worse than those located near it. Many of
these municipalities, especially those located northwest of Bogota, suffered dramatic declines in mean living standards. The few municipalities that achieved some gains did so as a result of increased oil royal-
ties and drug-related activities.

However, being farther from Bogota has not always meant
economic ruin. Figure 2.5 shows the spatial variation of average
municipal per capita income in 1973. Although in the early 1970s income was already higher in and around Bogota, it was not much lower
in the periphery and income per capita even went up slightly as we
move toward the periphery. Yet this situation changed dramatically in
the following two decades. The winners moved closer to Bogota, the

Map 2.1   Mexico: Per Capita Income by State

GDP per capita
(1995 pesos)

■	25,300–45,400 (6)
▨	21,000–25,300 (5)
▨	15,300–21,000 (4)
▨	12,500–15,300 (5)
☐	10,700–12,500 (4)
☐	8,300–10,700 (8)

1. Aguascalientes	9. Distrito Federal	17. Morelos	25. Sinaloa
2. Baja California	10. Durango	18. Nayarit	26. Sonora
3. Baja California Sur	11. Guanajuato	19. Nuevo León	27. Tabasco
4. Campeche	12. Guerrero	20. Oaxaca	28. Tamaulipas
5. Chiapas	13. Hidalgo	21. Puebla	29. Tlaxcala
6. Chihuahua	14. Jalisco	22. Querétano	30. Veracruz
7. Coahuila de Zaragoza	15. México	23. Quintana Roo	31. Yucatán
8. Colima	16. Michoacán	24. San Luis Potosí	32. Zacatecas

Source: Esquivel (2000).

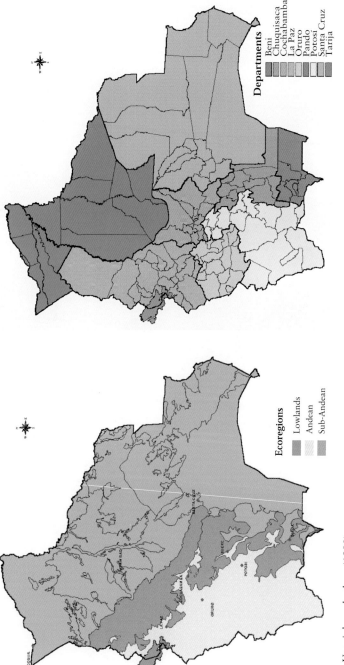

Map 2.2 Bolivia: Main Ecological Regions

Ecoregions

Lowlands
Andean
Sub-Andean

Source: Urquiola and others (1999).

Map 2.3 Bolivia: Departments and Provinces

Departments

Beni
Chuquisaca
Cochabamba
La Paz
Oruro
Pando
Potosí
Santa Cruz
Tarija

Source: Urquiola and others (1999).

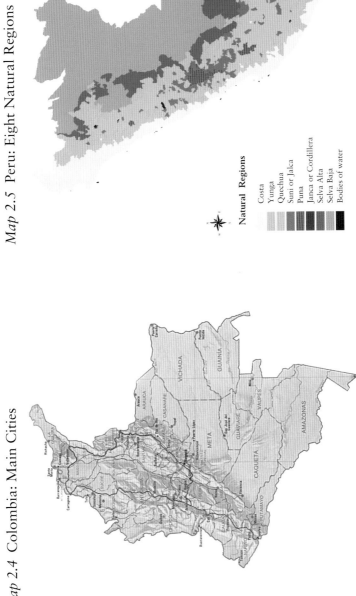

Map 2.5 Peru: Eight Natural Regions

Natural Regions

Costa
Yunga
Quechua
Suni or Jalca
Puna
Janca or Cordillera
Selva Alta
Selva Baja
Bodies of water

Source: Escobal and Torero (2000).

Map 2.4 Colombia: Main Cities

Source: Texas A&M University, Agricultural and Environment Safety,
http://www-aes.tamu.ed/CA/Colomap.htm

Map 2.6 Brazil: Geographical Distribution of Selected Diseases
(Morbidity rates: cases/population)

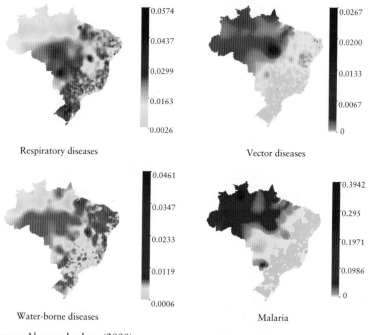

Respiratory diseases

Vector diseases

Water-borne diseases

Malaria

Source: Alves and others (2000).

losers away from it, and, as a result, the center of gravity of economic activity in Colombia moved toward the center. This spatial income concentration trend toward Bogota continued in the 1990s, in spite of the opening up and liberalization of trade processes that were intended to promote the economic development of ports and border regions (Fernández 1999).

What explains the change in the spatial distribution of economic activity in Colombia? Natural geography played a very important role, if not directly then at least indirectly. Thus, scale economies, transportation costs, and the integration of Colombia's dispersed regions were the main factors, all of them influenced by geography.

As mentioned, geographical barriers initially created a fragmented economic landscape in Colombia. Until recently, transport costs were such that a manufacturing firm located in Bogota could not compete in Barranquilla and vice versa. In the 1950s, a consensus emerged in Colombia about the urgency of massive investments in transportation infrastructure.[18] The idea was to connect the dispersed areas of the country in order to create a national market that would allow many industries to take advantage of economies of scale and scope. In the 1950s and 1960s, many roads were built and others completed. As a

Figure 2.5 Colombia: Municipalities per Capita Income Levels and Distance from Bogota

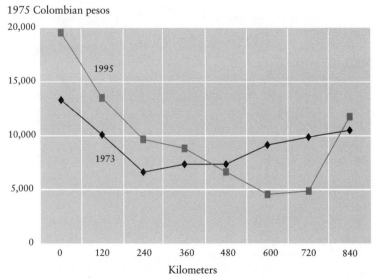

Source: Sánchez and Núñez (2000).

result, hitherto isolated zones gradually became interconnected and a national market finally came into being.

Increasingly, firms were able to compete nationally. To do so, many of them located near Bogota to take advantage of the large local markets. As a result, the center of gravity of the economy started moving toward the capital, causing in the process many casualties among the municipalities located on the periphery. Some municipalities lost manufacturing firms, others lost markets for their staple commodities, and the majority lost their most highly educated and talented people.

The Colombian experience seems logical for a closed economy in which firms serve mostly domestic markets. One would then expect that a reduction of barriers to international trade could reverse the trend toward centralization as firms would move near the coast to reduce transportation costs. However, the reduction of trade restrictions in Colombia in the early 1990s consolidated rather than attenuated the dominance of Bogota. Although the reasons are still debatable (and perhaps too little time has elapsed to draw definitive conclusions), it is clear that the advantages gained by Bogota over the last few decades are unlikely to disappear anytime soon. Not only is geography still influencing Colombia's patterns of regional development, but the legacy of past protectionist policies also lives on.

Peru

Only a handful of countries offer as many climatic zones and landscapes as Peru, with its rainforests, high mountain ranges, and dry deserts.[19] Peru contains 84 of the world's 104 ecological regions and 28 different climates. It also has one of the highest degrees of income inequality between regions in Latin America. The enormous diversity of its geography and the pronounced disparities in welfare across its different regions make Peru an intriguing case study for attempting to map out the interplay between geography and economic growth. Despite the fact that there have been many efforts to link Peru's geographical diversity to key issues such as the location of settlements or the establishment of administrative regions, very little has been done to analyze the links between its geographical diversity and development, economic growth, or poverty.

The only exception is the government's development of "poverty maps" to help target social programs. One of the most recent efforts in this regard is the design of poverty indices at the provincial and district levels by the Fondo Nacional de Compensación Social (FONCODES), the public agency in charge of poverty alleviation programs.

Although these maps are "geographical" in nature, no effort has been made to link them to geographical variables, such as trying to find out whether there is any kind of poverty trap due to the negative externalities of certain "geographical endowments."

This section attempts to ascertain the role of geographical variables, both natural and man-made, in explaining welfare differentials across regions of Peru, with an eye toward informing policy debates on what geographical factors matter to economic growth prospects at the micro level. The section closes with a closer look at the impact of geographical factors on economic inequality in Peru through the lens of regional disparities in health.

As is Bolivia, Peru is often divided into three distinct regions: the *costa* (coast and plains), the *sierra* (the Andean mountain range), and the *selva* (the jungle or Amazon). The entire coastal area of Peru (around 11 percent of its territory but with 49 percent of the total population) is one of the driest regions on the planet. Because of cold waters off the coast, the Andes Mountains, and winds from the south Pacific, the coast gets almost no rainfall. The country's mountainous areas comprise many separate ranges, accounting for 31 percent of Peruvian territory. Transportation through these mountains is usually difficult, especially in the southern Andes. Climatic conditions also make vast areas of the Peruvian Andes inhospitable. A large part of Peruvian territory (about 58 percent) lies within the Amazon Basin. Most of this area is covered by dense forest. Floods are common, and many areas are inundated for several months each year.

Many observers have argued that three regional categories are not sufficient to cover Peru's geographical diversity (Pulgar Vidal 1946; Peña Herrera 1986). Pulgar Vidal divides Peru into eight distinct "natural regions," as described in table 2.12 and depicted in map 2.5 (p. 101).

Geography and Economic Welfare

Table 2.13 shows that differences in per capita income between regions are larger in Peru than in Colombia, Brazil, Chile, and Mexico. Of all the countries studied by Fallon (1998), only Argentina has greater regional inequality than Peru. Furthermore, this dispersion is also very large within the different geographical regions of Peru.

These regional disparities are, at least in part, a reflection of differences in the provision of public infrastructure and public services. Although access to public goods and services has increased dramatically in rural areas of Peru in recent years, it continues to be biased in favor of urban areas. Only in education have rural areas been clearly favored by the recent expansion of government services.

Table 2.12 Eight Natural Regions of Peru

Region	Description
Costa or chala (coast or plain)	Territory below 500 m.o.s.l. (about 1,600 ft.) at the western side of the Andes. Mainly desertic.
Yunga (warm zone)	At both sides of the Andean mountain range, located between 500 and 2,300 m.o.s.l (1,600 ft. and 7,500 ft.) (on the western side) and 1,000 and 2,300 m.o.s.l (3,200 ft. and 7,500 ft.) (on the eastern side). Typically formed by valleys.
Quechua (temperate zone)	At both sides of the Andean mountain range, located between 2,300 and 3,500 m.o.s.l (7,500 ft. and 11,500 ft.). Typically formed by knolls and medium-steep hillsides.
Suni or jalca (cold lands)	At both sides of the Andean mountain range, located between 3,500 and 4,000 m.o.s.l. (11,500 ft. and 13,000 ft.). Typically formed by steep lands.
Puna (high-altitude plateau)	At the top of the Andean mountain range, located between 4,000 and 4,800 m.o.s.l. (13,000 ft. and 15,700 ft.). Just below the snowlands.
Janca or cordillera	At the top of the Andean mountain range, located between 4,800 and 6,768 m.o.s.l. (15,700 ft. and 22,190 ft.). This is not a continuous area. Usually no permanent settlements are found in this area (only 1 district capital of the 1,879 districts in Peru is located at an altitude higher than 4,800 m.o.s.l.).
Selva alta (high-altitude jungle)	Located at the eastern side of the Andean mountains, between 400 and 1,000 m.o.s.l. (1,300 ft. and 3,200 ft.). Mountainous forest with several valleys.
Selva baja (low-altitude jungle)	Located at the eastern side of the Andean mountains, below 400 m.o.s.l. (1,300 ft.).

Note: m.o.s.l. = meters over sea level.
Source: Escobal and Torero (2000), based on Pulgar Vidal (1946).

Of course, these disparities do not necessarily imply that regional differences in either infrastructure or natural conditions have a direct effect on welfare. If there are no impediments to migration, families will move according to their preferences and skills. Sooner or later, all families will move to the location that best suits them and, in equilibrium, all spatial differences will be explained on the basis of household characteristics. If this is the case, one can say that apparent geographical differences mask the fact that households with the same characteristics have the same welfare irrespective of their location.

Are Regional Disparities in Peru Due to Geography?

This question can be addressed by studying the effects of geographical variables on the levels and rates of growth of per capita expenditure at the provincial level (per capita expenditure is taken as a proxy for welfare). The question is whether geographical variables play a role even after controlling for some readily observable variables of the provinces, as in the case study of Colombia, as well as for the characteristics of each household (in a sample consisting of more than 3,600 households for the entire country).

Some of the variables considered for the provinces are similar to the ones used in the case study of Colombia: geographical variables, such as indicators of natural geography, urbanization, and distance to markets, on the one hand, and several variables that measure the provision of infrastructure and other public goods, on the other. The additional household attributes considered include the number of members of the household, their years of schooling, work experience, health status, and a series of other indicators of their assets. Most of these additional explanatory variables are influenced by income levels, and therefore their coefficient estimates are biased. However, the reason for their inclusion is not to assess the exact influence of these factors, but to test whether the geographical variables remain significant after their inclusion, which would prove the *direct* influence of geography on incomes and welfare.

Table 2.14 shows that the influence of geographical variables on welfare levels (as measured by expenditure) looks substantially higher when the role of household attributes is not taken into account. For instance, if only geographical variables are included, temperature appears to play a role in explaining expenditure levels. More specifically, expenditure declines for households located in regions with very low

Table 2.13 Dispersion of Regional Income per Capita in Selected Latin American Countries

Country	Year	Dispersion
Colombia	1989	0.358
Brazil	1994	0.424
Chile	1994	0.47
Mexico	1993	0.502
Peru	1997	0.561
Argentina	1995	0.736

Note: Unweighted coefficient variation.
Source: Escobal and Torero (2000), based on Fallon (1998) and Living Standards Measurement Surveys (1997).

Table 2.14 Peru: Determinants of per Capita Expenditure at the Household Level, 1994

Independent variable	[1]	[2]	[3]
Geography			
Altitude	0.272	−0.220	−0.123
	(0.93)	(−0.76)	(−0.54)
Temperature	0.106**	0.067**	0.038**
	(5.72)	(3.93)	(2.66)
Temperature	−0.002**	−0.001**	−0.001
squared	(−0.48)	(−2.80)	(−1.50)
Igneous rocks	0.107	0.041	0.113**
	(1.46)	(0.60)	(2.16)
Sedimentary rocks	−0.132**	−0.094**	−0.014
	(−3.19)	(−2.40)	(0.46)
Land depth	0.002**	0.003**	0.001
	(2.25)	(3.75)	(2.00)
Urbanization	0.392**	−0.062	−0.121
	(4.36)	(−0.61)	(−1.51)
Distance to provincial	−0.000	−0.001	−0.001
capital	(−0.50)	(−0.83)	(−1.20)
Urbanization *	0.697**	1.029**	0.607**
altitude	(1.98)	(2.97)	(2.21)
Infrastructure			
Per capita schools		0.360**	0.161
in province		(3.15)	(1.70)
Per capita medical		0.275	0.337
centers in province		(0.92)	(1.39)
Unsatisfied basic		−0.218**	−0.070**
needs in province		(−20.99)	(−7.11)
Private assets			
Household size			−0.116**
			(−27.57)
Schooling years			0.042**
(household head)			(14.38)
Schooling years			0.043**
(other members)			(13.00)
Potential labor			0.006**
experience			(8.14)
Household head			−0.013
gender			(−0.52)
Number of migrants			0.016**
			(2.16)
Spell of illness			0.001
(household head)			(0.06)

Independent variable	[1]	[2]	[3]
Savings			0.031**
			(4.560)
Value of durable			0.003
goods			(1.50)
Pseudo R^2	0.071	0.176	0.492
Observations	3,623	3,623	3,623

Note: All regressions include a constant term. t statistics are in parentheses.
** Significant at 5%.
Source: Escobal and Torero (2000).

or very high temperatures. Yet temperature loses much of its relevance when variables measuring the role of private assets are added to the specification. As expected, household characteristics such as education, labor experience, migration experience, and household size are strongly associated with expenditure levels. Interestingly, the percentage of households with unsatisfied basic needs in a province has a sizable effect on household expenditure, indicating the importance of critical public infrastructure, such as sanitation, water, telephone service, and electricity.

Table 2.15 shows a similar set of results, aimed at assessing the influence of geographical variables on the growth rates (instead of the levels) of per capita expenditure at the provincial level (growth rates refer to the period 1972–93). Again, three different groups of independent variables are used: geographical characteristics of the provinces, provincial infrastructure, and average household characteristics (for the last group of variables, we use the values as of 1972 to minimize endogeneity problems). If only geographical variables are included in the specification, altitude and longitude prove to be significant and economically relevant in explaining the growth of expenditure. The provinces located at higher elevations and those farther away from the coast tend to have slower rates of expenditure growth. But again, the addition of variables measuring the stocks of assets, both public and private, substantially reduces the importance of most natural geographical variables.

Interestingly, the residuals of all the regressions presented in table 2.15 show significant levels of spatial auto-correlation.[20] That is, fast-growing provinces tend to cluster together even after taking into account the effects of geography and household characteristics. This result suggests that either some key geographical variables or some spatially correlated household attributes have been omitted from our analysis. Regardless of the reason, this result implies that households

Table 2.15 Peru: Determinants of the per Capita Expenditure Growth Rate, 1972–93

Independent variable	[1]	[2]	[3]
Geography			
Altitude	−1.108**	−0.787*	0.262
	(−2.88)	(−2.09)	(0.68)
Latitude	−0.023	−0.031	−0.023
	(−1.33)	(−1.81)	(−1.22)
Longitude	−0.056**	−0.057**	−0.018
	(−3.12)	(−3.35)	(−1.21)
Soil slope	−0.001	0.002	0.003
	(−0.40)	(0.53)	(1.65)
Soil depth	−0.003	−0.002	0.002
	(−1.00)	(−0.85)	(1.00)
Igneous rock	−0.214	−0.294**	−0.320**
	(−1.70)	(−2.39)	(−3.20)
Metamorphic rock	0.073	0.054	−0.132
	(0.49)	(0.371)	(−1.08)
Temperature	−0.019	−0.005	−0.011
	(−1.91)	(−0.45)	(−1.27)
Infrastructure			
Unsatisfied basic needs in province		−0.056**	−0.022
		(−4.32)	(−1.31)
High basic needs			0.005
			(0.05)
School attendance rate in province			0.014**
			(4.77)
Household headed by women in province (%)			−0.011*
			(−2.18)
Working children in province (%)			0.053**
			(2.67)
Private assets			
Household size			0.078
			(0.59)
Household size growth			−0.262
			(−1.87)
Number of migrants			0.017
			(0.59)
Moran Index	0.109	0.101	0.082
Z-value	3.123	2.966	2.788
R² adjusted	0.122	0.195	0.486
Observations	190	190	190

Note: All regressions include a constant term. t statistics are in parentheses.
   *Significant at 10%.
  **Significant at 5%.
Source: Escobal and Torero (2000).

that share the same observable traits but live in different areas have different levels of welfare, and hence that there is ample justification for the social programs that use geographical targeting (Ravallion and Wodon 1997).

In summary, two main conclusions emerge. First, geographical variables (rainfall, temperature, elevation) do not appear to have a *direct* effect on household expenditure. This does not mean, however, that geography is not important, but rather that its influence on expenditure levels and growth differentials may come about through a geographically skewed provision of public infrastructure and through its effects on education and migration decisions by individuals. Furthermore, when the expected gain (or loss) in consumption from living in a geographical region (for example, coast) as opposed to living in another (for example, highlands) is measured, most of the difference in log per capita expenditure between the highland and the coast can be accounted for by the differences in infrastructure endowments and private assets. This could be an indication that the availability of infrastructure and basic social services (such as health and education) is limited by geography and therefore the more adverse geographical regions are the ones with less access to public infrastructure and social services, as will be discussed further for the case of health services.

Second, rich and poor households tend to cluster together in a way that cannot be explained by the spatial correlation of observable household attributes. Thus, although the direct evidence does not provide much confirmation that regional differences in Peru are driven by geographical differences, the dramatic clustering of poor households suggests that some unobserved geographical variables may play an important role.

An unforeseen implication of the data—one with relevance for policymakers—is the fact that adverse geographical externalities may provide incentives for migration. With respect to infrastructure development, for example, certain investments, such as education, are mobile with migration, while others are not. Therefore, it could be more profitable to invest in mobile infrastructure in the more adverse geographical regions to give people the necessary tools to migrate from these regions and therefore increase their probability of escaping the poverty trap.

Geography and Health

Regional inequalities in Peru are not restricted to poverty and consumption. Figure 2.6 shows that Peruvian regions also differ greatly in terms of health indicators. Child mortality in rural areas is twice as

Figure 2.6 Peru: Child Mortality Rates by Region and
Mother's Education, 1997

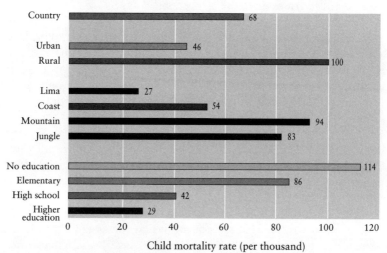

Child mortality rate (per thousand)

Source: Bitrán, Má, and Ubilla (2000).

high as in urban areas. Similarly, child mortality is much higher in the
mountainous and jungle regions than on the coast.

In theory, regional differences in health outcomes can be partially
driven by regional differences in natural geography. People living in
the humid regions carry greater risks of respiratory illness, people living in the mountains are more prone to cardiorespiratory illness, and
inhabitants of the jungle regions are exposed to a variety of multiple
infectious diseases (for example, leishmaniasis, bartenelosis, and yellow fever). But regional differences in health outcomes can also be
driven by differences in health provision and infrastructure. Table 2.16
shows, for example, that vaccination coverage differs greatly across
Peruvian regions, especially for poorer families. Whereas on the coast
42 percent of children whose mothers never completed primary education are vaccinated, in the mountains the corresponding figure is
only 14 percent.

Furthermore, regional differences in health outcomes can also be
driven by household characteristics. Some regions may exhibit better
health outcomes simply because they contain more middle-class and
wealthy families. In sum, regional differences in health can arise even
if natural geography does not play a role and health resources are
evenly distributed.

Table 2.17 shows the determinants of infant mortality rates at the provincial level[21] to examine whether geography indicators matter after controlling for the most obvious differences in health infrastructure and household attributes. If we include only geographical variables, a few empirical regularities are apparent: provinces located at lower elevations, southern latitudes, and near the coast tend to have lower rates of infant mortality. Once we expand our specification, elevation and latitude no longer have a clear association with infant mortality, but being close to the coast maintains its significance in all specifications.

Table 2.17 also shows that infant mortality rates are lower in provinces where illiteracy rates and the percentage of households without electricity are also low. Surprisingly, infant mortality rates appear to go up as the availability of health facilities increases. Given the possibility of reverse causality, this result should not be necessarily taken to imply that health expenditures have a perverse effect on health outcomes. In Peru, investments in ambulatory public facilities, particularly in health posts, have increased dramatically since the mid-1980s, and a guiding principle for the spatial allocation of the new facilities has been the provincial infant mortality rates. If the impact of these new investments occurs with a lag, the availability of health posts and

Table 2.16 Peru: Vaccination Coverage of Children under 5, 1987
(percent)

| | *Natural region* | | | |
Variable	Coast	Mountain	Jungle	Country
Vaccine type				
BCG	84.0	50.0	57.1	67.6
Polio	54.3	18.3	32.4	37.8
DPT	52.2	17.9	31.2	36.5
Measles	67.1	39.3	50.4	54.4
All types	46.4	13.0	27.6	31.3
Mother's education				
None	31.6	10.8	16.4	16.2
Some primary education	42.0	14.2	23.9	26.6
Complete primary education	50.6	25.7	40.2	42.2
Secondary education	60.2	35.8	60.5	55.7
Higher education	69.7	51.4	79.7	65.3

Note: BCG = Bacillus Calmette-Guerin; DPT = diphtheria, tetanus, pertussis.
Source: Bitrán, Má, and Ubilla (2000), based on Musgrove (1986).

Table 2.17 Peru: Determinants of Infant Mortality at the Provincial Level

Independent variable	[1]	[2]	[3]	[4]
Geography				
Altitude	0.010**	0.003**	0.001	0.001
	(8.28)	(2.77)	(1.23)	(0.72)
Rainfall	0.006**	−0.001	−0.002	−0.001
	(2.76)	(−0.41)	(−0.93)	(−0.67)
Distance to	2.353**	2.492**	3.473**	3.072**
the coast	(2.89)	(3.62)	(5.96)	(5.32)
Latitude	−2.675**	−2.010**	−1.735**	−0.963
	(−3.82)	(−3.26)	(−3.31)	(−1.75)
Temperature	−0.117	0.162	−0.054	0.016
	(−0.52)	(−0.87)	(−0.35)	(0.11)
Urbanization				
Urban		−0.393**	0.077	0.147
		(−9.07)	(1.02)	(1.90)
Population density		−0.001	−0.001	0.000
		(−0.52)	(−1.37)	(−0.23)
Infrastructure				
Illiteracy			1.040**	0.986**
			(6.98)	(6.48)
Households without		0.256**	0.244**	
electricity		(2.93)	(2.86)	
Health infrastructure				
(per 1,000 people)				
Doctors				−21.297**
				(−3.08)
Hospitals				−108.736
				(−1.05)
Centers and posts				24.918**
				(3.106)
Hospital beds				−0.119
				(−0.69)
R^2	0.622	0.743	0.823	0.836
Observations	190	190	190	190

Note: All regressions include a constant term. t statistics are in parentheses.
**Significant at 5%.
Source: Bitrán, Má, and Ubilla (2000).

the infant mortality rates will be negatively correlated, as effectively occurs in reality.

One main conclusion for health in Peru can be drawn from this analysis. The more one moves toward the coastal provinces, the better are the health conditions. Because this trend is not fully explained by differences in health infrastructure, urbanization, or educational levels, one can argue that it may well reflect the effects of some unobserved geographical characteristics on health outcomes. Of course, more research is needed to confirm this result and to determine the specific mechanisms through which geography affects health outcomes.

Brazil

Brazil's geography includes temperate savannas, rain forests, and arid coasts.[22] Average temperature increases dramatically as one moves from the densely populated southeast toward the sparsely populated northeast. Rainfall increases precipitously as one moves west toward the Amazon Basin. If, as many scientists predict, average global temperatures and rainfall increase over the next century, the consequences for health and development in Brazil could be particularly adverse. Understanding how environmental change can be expected to impact health is therefore of critical importance.

Health and Global Warming

Unpredictable and significant global climatic change challenges the ability of societies and institutions to respond adequately. Coastal development, agriculture, water supplies, health, and other societal systems are all taxed by large fluctuations in temperature and precipitation. Particularly with respect to health, there is a growing concern among physicians and climatologists that significant climatic changes could create even greater problems in areas of the world already struggling to confront existing illnesses, while introducing new problems in areas that are already relatively immune to certain diseases.

How can public health scientists predict and monitor the population health impact of this new challenge? Not surprisingly, the World Health Organization (1990) considers that the health consequences of global warming will be among the most pressing problems of the 21st century. It is necessary to detect and predict these effects early on so that countermeasures and coping mechanisms can be developed and introduced. With its unparalleled variety of climatic zones, Brazil makes an excellent laboratory for the study of these effects.

Depending on how emissions of greenhouse gases evolve in the future, over the next century the global mean temperature may increase by 1–4 degrees Celsius (1.8–7.2 degrees Fahrenheit). Sea level might rise by another 15–90 centimeters (6–35 inches), with a consequent increase in average evaporation and precipitation. In Brazil, a climatic change of this magnitude could have a substantial impact on health, both directly—by bringing about a sharp rise in heat-related mortality, for example—and indirectly by increasing the range of activity of vector-borne and infectious parasitic diseases.

The study described in this section was designed to shed light on the relationship between geography and health through the development of a model that predicts the impact of certain climatic variables on morbidity patterns for selected groups of diseases. More specifically, the study analyzes the direct effects of increases in temperature and rainfall, as well as indirect effects of other geographical/climatic variables such as altitude and distance from the sea, on respiratory, water-borne, and vector-transmitted diseases.[23] These diseases not only are known to be very sensitive to climatic changes, but also account for a sizable portion of all hospitalizations and deaths in Brazil. Data at the level of the municipality—the smallest government unit—are used.

Sensitivity to Climatic Factors

Higher temperatures increase the risk of respiratory diseases in a variety of ways. Cold weather increases susceptibility to respiratory infections, hot weather exacerbates the effects of air pollution, and thermal stress increases the risk of many respiratory conditions. According to Martens (1998), an increase in average temperature of 1 degree Celsius (1.8 degrees Fahrenheit) above the limit of thermal comfort can increase mortality due to respiratory diseases by as much as 10 percent.

Changes in temperature and rain patterns can also affect the incidence of infectious diseases transmitted through water. Water shortages in households, which may lead to the use of contaminated surface waters, are associated with higher incidence of infant diarrhea and salmonella, as well as typhoid fever in adults. Higher temperatures, which may increase the consumption of water and fruits, are also associated with the most common water-borne infections.

Rises in humidity and precipitation affect the proliferation and behavior of vectors and facilitate the viability and maturation of etiologic agents (McMichael and Haines 1997). High humidity enhances the metabolism of vectors, especially mosquitoes, accelerating the maturation of etiologic agents and making them infectious to human beings for longer periods. Low humidity, on the other hand, can dehydrate vectors, forcing the female to have more blood feedings (Curto de Casas and Carcavallo 1995). Similarly, abundant rains may wash away larvae, while scarce rains can reduce the collection of water necessary for larvae development.

As mentioned in chapter 1, temperature is strongly associated with the incidence of malaria. The ideal range of temperature for the transmission of malaria is between 20 and 27 degrees Celsius (60 and 80.6 degrees Fahrenheit). A rise in temperature of 3 degrees Celsius (5.4 degrees Fahrenheit) can increase the epidemic potential by 30 times in areas that present intermittent transmission, and up to three times in areas of endemic transmission (Alves and others 2000).

Importance for Public Health

Respiratory diseases are important causes of mortality and morbidity in Brazil, mainly among children under five years of age and the elderly. Respiratory diseases are responsible for 11 percent of all deaths and 15 percent of hospitalizations.

Prior to 1970, water-borne diseases were an important cause of mortality for children under five. The mortality from such diseases, however, has decreased steadily over the last two decades, mainly as a result of investments in potable water systems and sewage disposal. This positive trend notwithstanding, Brazil was affected by the recent reemergence of cholera in Latin America. The first case was recorded in April 1991 near the Peruvian border. In subsequent years, cholera quickly spread throughout the northern and northeastern regions of the country following the Amazonia fluvial basins. Approximately 50,000 cases were recorded in 1993 and 1994 during the peak of the epidemic. Although today cholera is under control, it still has enormous epidemic potential.

Vector-transmitted diseases are important causes of morbidity in Brazil. Malaria is one of the country's most important public health problems. In the early 1950s, there were about 8 million cases of malaria every year. Today malaria affects as many as 600,000 people per year. Dengue epidemics have occurred frequently during the last two decades. The first was in Roraima in 1982, affecting about 12,000 people. In 1986, there were epidemics in Rio de Janeiro, Ceará, and Alagoas. Incidence rates for cutaneous leishmaniasis are below 30 cases per 100,000 inhabitants in the south and southeast, but can be as high as 200 cases per 100,000 in some areas of the Amazon.

Geographical Distribution of Disease Morbidity

Map 2.6 (p. 102) shows the geographical distribution of morbidity rates for selected groups of diseases based on information for more than 4,000 Brazilian municipalities. Mortality and morbidity rates are very similar for all the disease groups under analysis.[24]

Respiratory diseases are common throughout the country, while water-borne diseases are more prevalent in the north and northeast, affecting mainly those municipalities close to fluvial and maritime ports. Vector-transmitted diseases in general and malaria in particular are highly concentrated in the north and some areas of the midwest.

Table 2.18 presents rates of hospitalization per 10,000 inhabitants in each Brazilian state. Hospitalization for respiratory diseases does not differ substantially among states. Hospitalization for water-borne diseases varies from below 17 cases per 10,000 inhabitants in São Paulo to nearly 100 cases in Pará. Hospitalizations for vector-borne diseases vary from 0.03 case per 10,000 inhabitants in Rio Grande do Sul to 43 cases in Acre.

Because information on hospitalization rates reflects only the occurrence of the most severe cases—and severity may vary across regions—differences in hospitalization rates are not necessarily indicative of differences in incidence. For vector-borne diseases, for example, the available information refers mainly to the more serious cases of malaria (and possibly a few cases of visceral leishmaniasis).

Measuring Climate Effects on Health

The substantial spatial variation of climate in Brazil allows for studying the effects of rain and precipitation on health outcomes. When data are used on morbidity at the municipal level for selected diseases, the observed correlation between morbidity and seasonal measures of rainfall is exploited, while controlling for other exogenous municipal characteristics that might influence health outcomes.

Morbidity (or disease incidence) is calculated as the number of reported cases of the disease divided by municipal population (as last measured in 1996 and 1991, respectively). In addition to temperature and precipitation, the explanatory variables include measures of average education, age structure, altitude, distance from the sea, and population density.

As in the case of Peru, there is a risk that temperature and rainfall may be picking up unobserved municipal attributes. For this reason, Alves and others (2000) also include dummies for six Brazilian regions (that is, the north, northeast, Minas Gerais, Rio-São Paulo, the

Table 2.18 Brazil: Hospitalization Rates per 10,000
Inhabitants, by Disease and State, 1996

State	Disease		
	Respiratory[a]	Water borne[b]	Vector borne[c]
Rondonia	201.18	65.33	37.34
Acre	141.48	55.68	43.02
Amazonas	96.25	32.92	17.39
Roraima	105.48	24.17	27.81
Pará	184.92	98.64	17.88
Amapá	112.84	39.43	35.90
Tocantins	246.99	70.88	8.39
Maranhão	241.19	69.33	2.92
Piauí	199.27	72.70	0.66
Ceará	193.52	78.56	0.45
Rio Grande do Norte	166.70	69.46	1.26
Paraíba	215.71	65.16	0.42
Pernambuco	173.22	61.91	0.53
Alagoas	195.11	92.67	0.44
Sergipe	141.59	34.36	0.84
Bahia	188.91	66.19	1.21
Minas Gerais	195.53	37.71	0.23
Espíritu Santo	164.51	33.26	0.10
Rio de Janeiro	143.08	26.38	0.08
São Paulo	126.57	16.73	0.11
Paraná	208.85	34.74	0.10
Santa Catarina	227.52	49.79	0.04
Rio Grande do Sul	250.17	40.88	0.03
Mato Grosso do Sul	165.86	50.29	0.03
Mato Grosso do Sul	228.97	46.60	3.50
Distrito Federal	334.68	18.89	0.00
Goiás	163.88	27.75	0.32

a. Groups according to the International Classification of Diseases (ICD 10).
b. Cholera, typhoid fever, and diarrhea.
c. Malaria, leishmaniasis, and dengue.
Source: Alves and others (2000).

south, and the central regions), as they believe that the inclusion of
regional dummies can attenuate this problem by eliminating all possible biases coming from unobserved regional attributes. It should
be mentioned, however, that the use of regional dummies comes at
the cost of ignoring the large climatic variation between Brazilian
regions. To estimate the effects of climate on the incidence of the
selected diseases, they use a Tobit model, which is the logical choice

given that many municipalities report no hospitalizations for the disease under analysis, especially for water- and vector-borne diseases. Marginal effects for the variables of interest discriminating by region are reported.[25]

Figure 2.7 shows the effects of temperature on respiratory diseases. Although the effect of annual temperature is very small, spring and summer temperatures are clearly associated with higher incidence rates of respiratory diseases. Fall and winter temperatures, on the other hand, are associated with lower incidence rates. In sum, more pronounced weather swings (hot summers followed by cold winters) will tend to increase the incidence of respiratory diseases.

Figure 2.8 shows the effects of rainfall and population density on the incidence of water-borne diseases. Higher rainfall is associated with lower morbidity rates, particularly in the north and northeast regions. In the north, an additional inch (2.54 centimeters) of rainfall per year reduces incidence rates by more than seven cases per 10,000 people—a 20 percent fall in some states. Figure 2.9 shows the effects of temperature on the incidences of water-borne diseases. Although average annual temperatures are slightly beneficial, summer temperatures appear to be very harmful, particularly in the north and northeast.

Figure 2.10 shows that increased spring rainfall raises the incidence of vector-borne diseases in both the north and central regions. Increased winter rain, on the other hand, reduces vector-related morbidity in the north. Figure 2.11 shows that higher fall temperatures seem to be beneficial all over the country, whereas higher winter temperatures seem to be harmful in the north and central regions. These complicated seasonal patterns are likely to be related to the life cycle of the anopheles mosquito.[26]

Three main conclusions emerge from analysis of climatic effects on health in Brazil. First, the effects of temperature and precipitation on health outcomes differ greatly from one region to another. Second, these effects depend on complex interactions between rainfall and temperature, and even among climate, population settlement patterns, and education. And last, the size and seasonal pattern of climatic effects differ greatly among the various groups of diseases considered.

The job of scientists has only begun and the challenge for Brazilian policymakers is great. The influence of climatic variables on health outcomes is evident, but the complexities of the interaction defy clear and universal conclusions even when analyzed statically at a given point in time. This complicates the already daunting task of preparing for the effects of climatic change over time.

Figure 2.7 Bounds of Marginal Effects of Temperature on Respiratory Diseases

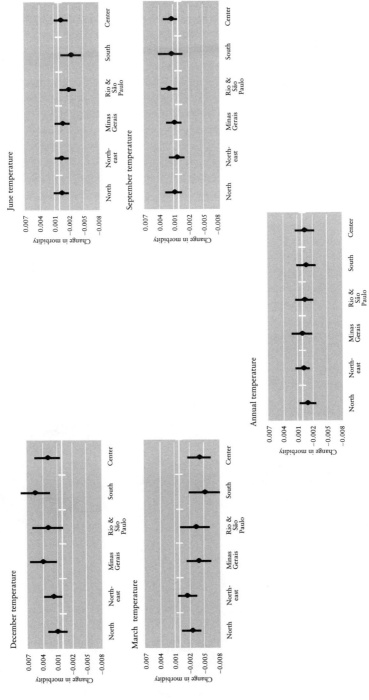

Source: Alves and others (2000).

Figure 2.8 Bounds of Marginal Effects of Rainfall and Population Density on Water-Borne Diseases

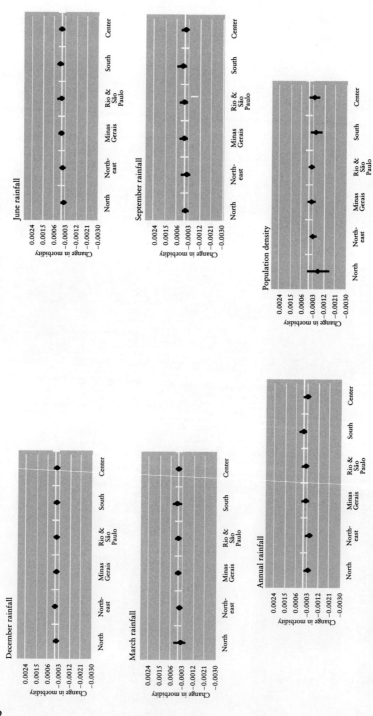

Source: Alves and others (2000).

Figure 2.9 Bounds of Marginal Effects of Temperature on Water-Borne Diseases

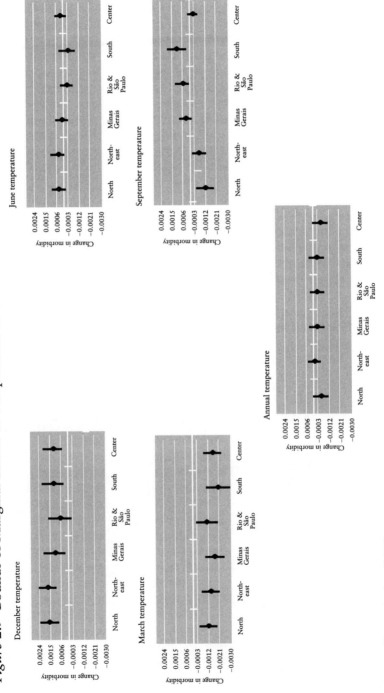

Source: Alves and others (2000).

Figure 2.10 Bounds of Marginal Effects of Rainfall and Population Density on Vector-Borne Diseases

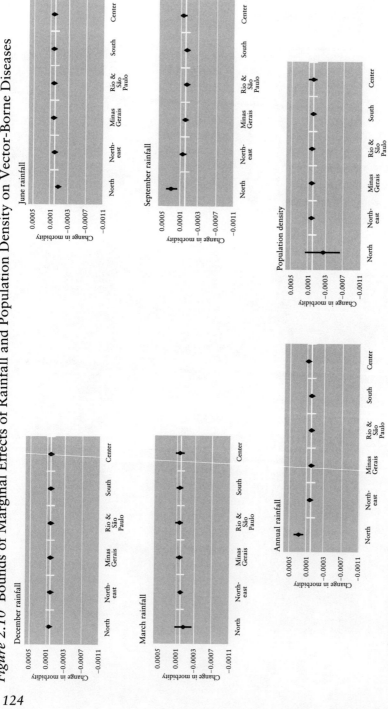

Source: Alves and others (2000).

Figure 2.11 Bounds of Marginal Effects of Temperature on Vector-Borne Diseases

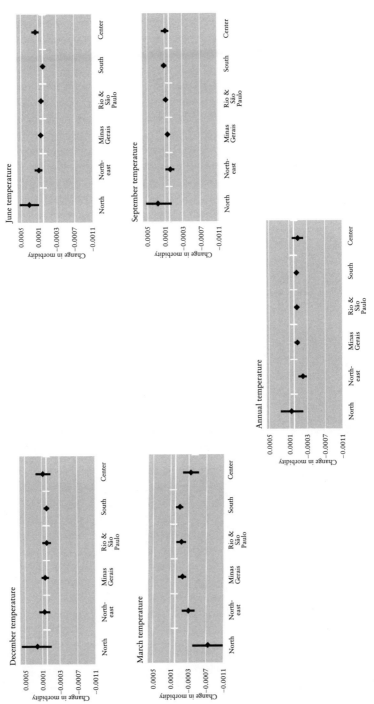

Source: Alves and others (2000).

125

Conclusions

The major conclusion that can be drawn from the results of this chapter is that the connections between geography and development are not as straightforward as suggested by a quick glance at the cross-country evidence presented in the previous chapter. First, the different mechanisms of causality often interact with each other in complex and unpredictable ways. Second, institutional and historical forces often redirect, reinforce, or even undermine the effects of geography. The following are examples of the contrast between the cross-country evidence presented in chapter 1 and the more-detailed evidence presented in this chapter:

• The evidence from Bolivia shows that tropical climates do not always spell stagnation. The impressive growth of Santa Cruz and its surrounding areas makes it clear that deleterious climatic conditions are not an insurmountable hurdle. Santa Cruz has a solid and diversified economy that is bound to grow in the years to come.

• The cases of Colombia and Mexico show that port cities and coastal areas, despite their obvious advantages for international trade, do not always have the edge over central locations. Political centralization and inward-looking economic policies can turn relatively isolated central locations into powerful economic centers. Moreover, their advantages tend to persist long after the policies that gave rise to them are dismantled. In a related point, the Mexican and Colombian experiences show that the positive connection between economic growth and a country's coastal population—a key result of chapter 1—may reflect not so much (or not only) the effects of higher transport costs on growth as the effects of protectionist economic policies.

• The evidence from Brazil shows the complex connection between health and climatic conditions (rainfall and temperature in this case). This connection depends heavily on the type of disease and on the seasonal behavior of the climatic variables. The effect of an inch of rainfall in June is not the same as the effect of an inch of rainfall in December—and these effects are in turn different depending on whether we are looking at water- or vector-borne diseases. Such intricacies are often lost in cross-country studies, which rely more on annual averages and aggregated health indicators.

• Mexico shows that institutions can carry the influence of geography across decades and even centuries. The geographical and institutional circumstances encountered by the first European colonizers greatly influenced the types of institutional arrangements adopted during colonial times. These initial institutions have in turn greatly influenced the path of institutional change in Mexico. Thus, the current political institutions of many areas of central and southern Mexico can be understood only as the legacy of geographical circumstances from times long past.

• Finally, all the studies in this chapter show that migration may mitigate but does not erase the effects of geography, which in turn points to the presence of substantial migration costs (related perhaps to cultural barriers and the specific status of a country's human capital). All the countries under analysis showed substantial differences in per capita income among provinces or states, albeit much smaller than those among countries of the world. In sum, although migration surely equalizes spatial differences in living conditions, it does not erase the influence of space on living conditions.

Geography influences development, but not always in the same way. The international patterns identified in chapter 1 are useful starting points for analysis but are not hard-and-fast rules. The case studies presented here are chock-full of exceptions to the rules. And that is good news. It means the future of countries is not etched in the stone of their mountains or bound by the equator or seared into their people by the heat of the tropics. The diversity of these cases does not refute the basic premise that geography matters. It does, however, prove that geography is not destiny.

Notes

1. The Latin American Research Network studies that are the basis for this chapter are available on the Internet at http://www.iadb.org/RES.

2. This section on Mexico is based on Esquivel (2000) and Blum and Díaz Cayeros (2002).

3. Another peculiar characteristic of Mexico's poorest states is that they have many political jurisdictions (municipalities) per square mile. This can be explained by either their more rugged landscape (mobility is lower, which facilitates rent extraction by local bosses) or the prevalent institutions of land tenure (the administration of *ejidos* requires more structural density).

4. The small sample size prevents the inclusion of all the groups at the same time to ensure that the one-group associations are not proxying in part for the other groups.

5. These states are Colima, Guerrero, Hidalgo, México, Morelos, Nayarit, Oaxaca, and Puebla. However, these results would imply that it is better to live in the middle of the desert or in an area under constant torrents than in areas with more moderate rainfall. This suggests that rainfall is probably proxying for other variables that are responsible for that pattern.

6. Convergence rates are computed on the basis of the following equation:

$$\frac{y_{i,t} - y_{i,t-\tau}}{\tau} = \alpha - [1 - \exp(-\beta)]\, y_{i,t-\tau} + u_{i,t}$$

where $y_{i,t}$ is the log of GDP per capita of state i in period t, $u_{i,t}$ is an error term, and β is the rate of convergence. This expression implies that the change in per capita income is greater the lower the initial income. Greater values of β indicate that poorer states grow on average at faster rates.

7. This section on Bolivia is based on Urquiola and others (1999) and Morales and others (2000).

8. This and related figures are based on data from the 1950, 1976, and 1992 censuses. Unless stated otherwise, all the analysis below focuses on the 1950–92 period.

9. Although Bolivia currently has 112 provinces, the analysis below concentrates on only 99 of them to allow comparison with the 1976 census data. Achieving a consistent set of geographical units is feasible, mainly because all new provinces originated from the split of previously single provinces into two new ones.

10. The UBN index is based on four different groups of variables: (a) access to housing (number of occupants per room and quality of construction materials); (b) access to basic services (water, sewage, electricity, type of cooking fuel); (c) education (attainment, school enrollment of children, and literacy); and (d) health and social security.

11. Morales and others (2000) show that poverty rates are positively associated with soil erosion, especially in those provinces where agriculture constitutes a large portion of local production.

12. This section on Colombia draws partly from Sánchez and Núñez (2000).

13. Data on municipal GDP are not available in Colombia, so tax receipts from property and commerce taxes are used here to proxy for income. We compute per capita income by first calculating the share of each municipality in the total tax revenues of a particular department and then multiplying such share by the departmental GDP (Sánchez and Núñez 2000).

14. Geographical variables were computed using primary sources. The procedure used to obtain the index of soil suitability is a case in point. The three steps followed were to (a) create digital soil maps; (b) calculate, for every municipality, the area of each type of soil; and (c) estimate, for every municipality, a soil quality index using a previously constructed ranking of the production suitability of each type of soil. A similar procedure was followed to compute the index of water availability and the river and road densities (Sánchez and Núñez 2000).

15. It should be noticed that this regression attempts to explain growth *after* 1973 as a result of a number of factors *as of* 1973. By doing so, we try to avoid the endogeneity bias resulting from the influence of growth on the explanatory variables.

16. Malaria was originally more prevalent in the lower valley of the Magdalena and Cauca Rivers and along both the Pacific and Caribbean coasts (Currie 1950, p. 179).

17. Results are not shown in the table but are available in the case study by Sánchez and Núñez (2000).

18. Currie (1950) argued that the "lack of a unified transportation system in Colombia is one of the main factors contributing to the high costs of manufacturing goods" and a primary contributing factor "in limiting industrial markets."

19. This section on Peru is based on Escobal and Torero (2000) and Bitrán, Má, and Ubilla (2000).

20. We use the Moran I statistic to measure spatial correlation. This indicator is akin to the Durbin-Watson statistic that is commonly used to test autocorrelation in time series data. See Escobal and Torero (2000) for an in-depth analysis of the spatial correlation of Peruvian social indicators.

21. Although infant mortality rates (IMRs) in Peru are available at the provincial level, the country's National Statistical Institute has imputed the IMRs to provinces using regression analysis on some departmental values. Geographical variables are also available at the provincial level, with the exception of temperature, which is available only for departments. Some health-related information exists down to only the departmental level. Finally, information on households and individuals, such as access to basic public services and education, exists for both departments and provinces. See Bitrán, Má, and Ubilla (2000) for a comprehensive description of health information in Peru.

22. This section on Brazil is based on Alves and others (2000).

23. Respiratory diseases include pneumonia, bronchopneumonia, and obstructive diseases (asthma, emphysema, and chronic bronchitis). Water-borne diseases include gastroenteritis, typhoid fever, and cholera. Vector-borne diseases include malaria, dengue, and leishmaniasis.

24. Information on mortality comes from the system of mortality information (SIM) managed by the Ministry of Health. Information on hospitalization comes from the hospital information system (DATASUS). For malaria and cholera, the information comes from the Brazilian Center for the Control of Epidemics (CENEPI). See Alves and others (2000) for a thorough description of the data sources.

25. Standard errors for the marginal effects were bootstrapped from the variance-covariance matrices of the estimated parameters.

26. The effects of rainfall and temperature on malaria are almost identical to those of vector-borne diseases as a whole (see Alves and others 2000).

3

Policies to Overcome the Limitations of Geography

GEOGRAPHY MAY BE LARGELY IMMUTABLE, but its impact on an economy and a society is not. The right policies or technological developments can overcome many geographical obstacles and help exploit geographical advantages.

Tackling geographical problems has important "public good" aspects: investments in disease control, roads, or disaster mitigation typically benefit whole regions rather than particular individuals. But making these investments at the level that is socially desirable requires coordination between the government and other institutions. On an individual level, a citizen who contributes to these investments will not necessarily capture the benefits that he or she is contributing to society as a whole, and thus is less likely to want to contribute what is needed. No individual would like the task of controlling a dispersed disease vector, for example, and yet everyone benefits when each person contributes a small amount to the eradication of the disease. The sharing of the burden requires coordination and the creation of market-based incentives.

Regional Development

Latin America has large concentrations of people in geographically difficult environments such as the highlands of Central America and the Andean region, the Brazilian northwest, and Haiti. In all the countries studied in chapter 2, these geographically disadvantaged regions have higher levels of poverty, worse health conditions, lower educational achievements, and more limited access to infrastructure and basic services.

If areas adjacent to geographically disadvantaged areas develop rapidly, some of the problems of these difficult environments may be spontaneously solved by migration to the dynamic neighboring regions. For many people, migration is the only way to escape the constraints of geography. Nevertheless, spontaneous and unassisted migration can result in simply transferring poverty elsewhere.[1] Moreover, the persistence of poverty in these population centers indicates that migration is not a lasting solution. Population growth is often higher in poor, geographically disadvantaged regions, offsetting the benefits of outmigration. Finally, massive migration to economic centers and to some coastal areas might cause additional problems, such as increased vulnerability to natural disasters or uncontrolled urbanization. Avoiding such adverse effects of migration requires closely monitoring migration patterns, providing assistance to urban settlers, creating incentives for settlements in safe areas, and adapting city and land use planning.

Developing remote and poorer regions represents a difficult challenge for public policy. Experiences in developed and developing countries indicate that state-driven regional development efforts are rarely successful. Regional development agencies usually have trouble putting together the complex coordination necessary to get economic networks established in places where this has not occurred spontaneously. In Brazil, for example, the strategy of opening up the Amazonian frontier for poor settlers from the northeast has caused major environmental damage, had limited economic success, and exacerbated problems of tropical disease. Smaller-scale regional development initiatives executed by grassroots organizations in coordination with local authorities have a much better record, such as the Plan Sierra in the Dominican Republic (de Janvry and Sadoulet 2000).

Diversifying economic activities through tourism development, environmental conservation programs, or duty-free zones can help the development of disadvantaged zones, whose economic activity is generally agricultural. As shown in chapter 2, overspecialization in coffee has brought stagnation to many Colombian municipalities. In general, regions with more diversified economies are more likely to develop as their dependency on a single market or weather patterns diminishes. Even with lower yields, disadvantaged areas should be able to profit from international trade because of the cheap price of land and labor. But a key hurdle to the development of higher value-added agriculture and processed foods in many disadvantaged areas is the liberalization of agricultural trade. Another obstacle is the underutilization of existing natural endowments. Poorer households have less access to land because of inequality in asset ownership and the failure of land rental markets (de Janvry and Sadoulet 2000).

Active approaches to reducing geographical disparities through infrastructure investments can be effective in spurring growth. The construction of interregional infrastructure has an enormous impact on spatial development patterns, as seen in Santa Cruz in Bolivia, where growth increased in part because of construction of a highway to Cochabamba, another major urban agglomeration (see chapter 2). However, infrastructure-led development of disadvantaged areas can be enormously difficult. The nature of isolated areas makes extension of infrastructure to them more expensive, so the benefits to their residents must be large to support these costs. If the goal is to bring industry and white-collar services to these areas, the problem becomes the strong synergies, or economies of agglomeration, attached to these activities. These synergies make returns to new infrastructure investments higher in cities that are more accessible and already well connected. Bringing industrial and service activities to an isolated area is a chicken and egg problem—that is, firms do not want to set up there unless the infrastructure and services are already in place and other firms are also going to establish themselves there. Cost recovery for the infrastructure is not possible unless it attracts a good number of firms. To get this all moving simultaneously is expensive and risky, and governments that have attempted it have poor track records (Richardson and Townroe 1986).

Less-ambitious infrastructure projects that build on local strengths rather than initiating new sectors from scratch are likely to be more successful. A "basic needs" approach to infrastructure may be the most effective way to reduce poverty in geographically disadvantaged regions, and may also have a higher economic rate of return than large-scale infrastructure projects. Rudimentary feeder roads, electricity, and telecommunications are needed to integrate isolated regions into the rest of the economy. New technologies for microelectricity generation and stand-alone telecommunications links may also prove most cost-effective. Moreover, investments in basic infrastructure in disadvantaged areas, such as education, water, electricity, and sanitation, might have higher returns than upgrading facilities in areas already well equipped.

Providing cost-effective infrastructure in isolated regions is easier said than done, however. Centralized provisioning is not always the best method, since infrastructure investment projects and the services they provide are inherently located in and serve particular areas, customers, and interests. Some form of decentralization is granted for most infrastructure investment and services, but the precise form it takes may depend on a number of factors.

While a basic needs approach should guide infrastructure investment decisions for geographically disadvantaged areas, the evidence presented in chapter 1 suggests that access to international markets should be the primary criterion for investments in roads, ports, railways, and airports. Of course, the potential benefit of these investments depends on a number of variables, and overexpenditure is always a risk. Few of those investments can be profitable in the absence of adequate trade and macroeconomic policies to encourage producers to pursue international integration over the long term. But the potential benefit of a trade liberalization policy may in turn be severely limited by lack of infrastructure. Internal transportation bottlenecks can prevent the development of potentially successful exporting sectors, especially primary ones, while high value-added imports may soar. A basic needs approach should also consider the risks associated with natural disasters by incorporating measures to minimize the destruction of private and public infrastructure and prevent sudden cutoffs from markets. Similarly, governments should focus efforts on reinstating access to markets in the aftermath of disasters by rebuilding critical infrastructure.

Finally, a basic needs approach to infrastructure should also be based on the principle that adequate maintenance of basic services is more important than building new facilities that are usually more expensive to run and keep up. The lack of adequate infrastructure in poor regions is more often due to poor maintenance policies than to insufficient expenditure. As has been emphasized by the World Bank (1994), new economic and political institutions and incentives, particularly if they are not decentralized in some fashion, usually lead to costly and inefficient new investments. A fraction of those same resources could often provide better services were they devoted to maintenance.

Research and Technology

New telecommunications technologies and the Internet may also play a future role in reducing the significance of geographical barriers. Information and communications technologies can enhance the efficiency of firms and encourage market development by lowering transaction costs in the region (Bedi 1999). Areas where transaction costs are very high, such as in remote and sparsely inhabited rural regions, should strongly benefit from these technological changes.

Of course, these advances will benefit already accessible locations as well. And despite the dramatically lower user cost of modern telecommunications, a large initial investment in infrastructure will be required. Finally, technological advances do not automatically bring dramatic progress. One might have expected similar revolutionary change in access from the telephone, but it has not made geographical barriers obsolete. These points reveal that new technologies could actually exacerbate existing inequalities unless public policies ensure that remote areas are not left out of the information technology revolution. The use of new technologies could bring dramatic improvements, for example, in disaster-prone areas. More effective emergency communications would lessen the human and economic costs associated with disasters by providing populations with early warnings and by facilitating communication with isolated areas in the aftermath of disasters.

Although geography is largely immutable, the prevalence of disease in particular climates can clearly be reduced, and low yields in tropical agriculture can be improved. In these two areas, research and technological innovation could radically change existing constraints on human development. In the case of health, direct action is required because rising income levels per se will not be enough to resolve the problems in this area. For some diseases, there are few affordable and effective treatment and control strategies, while for others the means of conquering the disease are well known but require a major education and mobilization effort. A prime example of the former is malaria. Vector control in the worst areas is at best a holding action, and the medicines being used are rapidly losing their effectiveness because of drug resistance. Vaccines are still many years away because of shortages in funding and the extraordinary complexity of the pathogen and its life cycle. Tropical diseases do not get the benefits of spillovers from biomedical and pharmaceutical research in the developed countries because there are no significantly large tropical developed countries. The tropical countries are too poor to offer an attractive stand-alone market to induce pharmaceutical firms to invest in tropical disease research.

Similar problems are faced in developing agricultural technology for soils and products characteristic of the tropics. Almost all scientific research and development, and hence most technological advances, occur in the developed world. At least some of these advances have the potential to be adapted to poor tropical countries, but significant hurdles must be overcome because of the differences in the biological process in the tropics.

In the industrial world, more and more cutting-edge scientific research in health and agriculture is being carried out by large private firms rather than in government and academic research institutes. These firms have no financial incentive to invest in similar research on tropical problems. Since developing country consumers cannot afford to pay premium prices for new drugs and vaccines, they are not a profitable market.

At the same time as the tropics are being left out of the revolution in corporate scientific research, public funding for research on tropical agriculture and disease has been declining. The research and development budget of the entire system of research institutes that constitutes the Consultative Group on International Agricultural Research (CGIAR) is less than half that of one life-sciences multinational, Monsanto (Sachs 1999, p. 19).

Despite these limitations, a new era of rapid advances in biology has allowed for promising applied research on the obstacles to tropical agriculture. Tropical agricultural research, most of it public, has had high rates of return in Latin America. Table 3.1 reports findings of a study by Echeverría (1990) that assessed research on different crops in different countries using different methodologies, yet whose findings were uniformly and strikingly high. Of the 58 rates of return, only 4 are below 15 percent per year, with an average of 57 percent and a median of 44 percent. These huge returns on what little research investment has been made suggest that not enough agricultural research has been undertaken and that major hurdles may be impeding it.[2]

Even if agricultural research did not have such high economic returns, investing in agricultural improvements can still be justified in terms of its impact on the poor. The near-term welfare of more than half the households in low-income countries (69 percent of the labor force in 1990), and an even higher proportion of the poorest households, still depends on agriculture (World Bank 1997, p. 220).

The rate of return to investing in tropical medical research is difficult to calculate, and in any case is secondary to the principal benefit of such research, which is better human health and welfare. Not surprisingly, the level of funding for research on tropical health problems is pitifully low. The prime example is malaria, one of the most deadly tropical diseases in the world. An estimated 2.4 billion people are at risk worldwide, with 300 million to 500 million clinical cases and 1.5 million to 2.5 million deaths per year. Yet because of the lack of market incentives, there is essentially no malaria research by private pharmaceutical firms. Total worldwide research funding was only $84 million in 1993, much of it by the military of wealthy countries concerned about the readiness of their soldiers overseas (Welcome Trust 1999).

In spite of this limited funding and research, Latin America overall has better health than would be predicted by its income levels, especially for a region that is highly tropical.[3] A series of successful control programs and strong public health institutions such as the Pan American Health Organization—many supported early on by the Rockefeller Foundation—have had a remarkable impact on the disease burden in the region. These programs have included control of yellow

Table 3.1 Rates of Return to Agricultural Research and Extension in Latin America

Author	Year	Country	Commodity	Period	Annual rate of return (%)
Ayer	1970	Brazil (São Paulo)	Cotton	1924–67	77
Barletta	1970	Mexico	Crops	1943–63	45–93
			Wheat		90
Elias (revised by Cordomi)	1971	Argentina (EEAT-Tucuman)	Sugar cane	1943–63	33–49
Hines	1972	Peru	Maize	1954–67	35–55
Patrick and Kehrberg del Rey (revised by Cordomi)	1973	Brazil (Eastern)	Aggregate	1968	0
	1975	Argentina (EEAT-Tucuman)	Sugar cane	1943–64	35–41
Monteiro	1975	Brazil	Cocoa	1923–85	19–20
Fonseca	1976	Brazil	Coffee	1933–95	17–27
Hertford and others	1977	Colombia	Rice	1957–80	60–82
			Soybeans	1960–80	79–96
			Wheat	1927–76	11–12
			Cotton	1953–72	0
Wennergren and Whittaker	1977	Bolivia	Sheep	1966–75	44
			Wheat		–48
Scobie and Posada	1978	Colombia	Rice	1957–64	79–96
Moricochi	1980	Brazil (São Paulo)	Citrus	1933–85	18–28

(Table continues on the following page.)

137

Table 3.1 (continued)

Author	Year	Country	Commodity	Period	Annual rate of return (%)
Avila	1981	Brazil (R.G. do Sul)	Irrigated rice	1959–78	83–119
		Brazil (Central)			83–87
		Brazil (N. Coast)			92–107
		Brazil (S. Coast)			111–115
		Brazil (Frontier)			114–119
Cruz and others	1982	Brazil	Physical capital	1974–81	53
			Total investment	1974–92	22–43
Evenson	1982	Brazil	Aggregate	19??–74	69
Ribeiro	1982	Brazil (Minas Gerais)	Aggregate	1974–94	69
			Cotton		48
			Soybeans		36
Yrarrazaval and others	1982	Chile	Wheat	1949–77	21–28
			Maize	1940–77	32–34
Avila and others	1983	Brazil (EMBRAPA)	Human capital	1974–96	22–30
Cruz and Avila	1983	Brazil (EMBRAPA)	Aggregate	1977–91	38
Martinez and Sain	1983	Panama (IDIAP-Caisan)	Maize	1979–82	188–332
Ambrosi and Cruz	1984	Brazil (EMBRAPA-CNPT)	Wheat	1974–90	59–74
Avila and others	1984	Brazil (South Central)	Aggregate	1974–96	38
Feijoo (revised by Cordomi)	1984	Argentina (INTA)	Aggregate	1950–80	41
Pinazza and others	1984	Brazil (São Paulo)	Sugar cane	1972–82	35
Roessing	1984	Brazil (EMBRAPA-CNPS)	Soybeans	1975–82	45–62
Silva	1984	Brazil (São Paulo)	Aggregate		60–102

Author	Year	Country/Region	Crop	Period	Rate
Ayres	1985	Brazil	Soybeans	1955–83	46–69
		Brazil (Parana)			51
		Brazil (R.G. do Sul)			51–53
		Brazil (S. Catarina)			29–31
		Brazil (São Paulo)			23–24
Muchnik	1985	Latin America	Rice	1968–90	17–44
Norton and others	1987	Peru (INIPA)	Aggregate	1981–2000	17–38
			Rice		17–44
			Maize		10–31
			Wheat		18–36
			Potatoes		22–42
			Beans		14–24
Echevarria and others	1988	Uruguay	Rice	1965–85	52
Evenson	1988	Paraguay	Crops	1988	75–90
Luz Barbosa	1988	Brazil (EMBRAPA)	Aggregate	1974–97	40
Evenson and da Cruz	1989	South America (PROCISUR)	Wheat	1979–88	110
			Soybeans		179
			Maize		191
Average					57
Median					44

Source: Echeverria (1990, table 1).

fever in the early 1940s, the elimination of the malaria-carrying *Anopheles gambiae* mosquito in Brazil in the 1930s, and hookworm control in the 1920s. The Rockefeller Foundation also supported agricultural research in Mexico in the 1940s that eventually became CYM-MIT, bringing elements of the Green Revolution to Latin America. The foundation funded the respected CIAT agricultural research institute in Colombia and others in the region.

Although many of these health and agricultural organizations and initiatives continue to contribute influential research, some of the technological challenges posed by geographical and ecological conditions in Latin America today require investments beyond their reach. Besides, they may lack the comparative advantage to develop certain products or technologies developed by private high technology firms.

With regard to malaria, for example, Jeffrey Sachs has suggested a coordinated pledge by rich countries promising an attractive market to the firm that succeeds in developing the vaccine (Sachs 1999, pp. 17–20). A guaranteed minimum purchase price or fixed amount per dose would be paid when the vaccine actually exists. Similar pledges could spur cures for other diseases such as tuberculosis, or for the development of crop varieties or agricultural technologies adequate to the geographical and climatic conditions of the poor countries. A huge step has already been taken with the creation of the Global Fund to Fight AIDS, Tuberculosis, and Malaria. Pledges from government and private donors amount to more than US$2 billion. The purpose of the fund is to attract, manage, and disburse additional resources through a new public-private partnership aimed at reducing the incidence of infection and mortality due to these diseases. The fund will provide grants to public, private, and nongovernmental organizations to carry out locally sustainable projects.

Of course, there are other forms of international cooperation that could promote these advances. Depending on the scale, the type of externalities of the problem, and the likely costs of finding a solution, cooperation might be most effective at the subregional, regional, or global level. It may also require the involvement of international organizations, some of which could play a role in identifying global and regional priorities in health and agriculture and in mobilizing private sector research and development.

Information and Market Signals

Because many Latin American countries are so geographically diverse, different regions within a country may offer very marked comparative advantages or disadvantages for certain activities. The yield from investments in infrastructure or health care interventions, for example, may differ dramatically from one zone to another and between different-size cities and towns because of population settlement patterns. Disaster prevention efforts may be best directed to certain locations because they are more prone to hurricanes, floods, or earthquakes.

Keeping these geographical variables in mind when developing a range of economic and social policies requires good information, which is unlikely to be provided by the market of its own accord given the nature of information as a public good. Some of the larger Latin American countries have geographical and statistical institutes primarily devoted to gathering information on the human and geographical factors that affect development. The Instituto Brasileiro de Geografia (IBGE) and Mexico's Instituto Nacional de Estadística, Geografía e Informática (INEGI) enjoy international prestige for their technical and analytical ability. Nevertheless, such efforts are just beginning in many countries where the agencies responsible are not guided by clear economic and social policy objectives and do not provide significant support to policymakers. Hence, geographical considerations are often not factored into decisions on infrastructure investment, allocation of health care expenditures, or plans for urban development, settlement, or disaster prevention.

The gathering, processing, and dissemination of geographical information must be the responsibility of central bodies, since they are complex tasks that require considerable costs, offer major economies of scale, and give rise to significant externalities. There may even be a need for supranational agencies to deal with phenomena that transcend national borders, such as hurricanes or El Niño. Still, a great deal of information related to geography can be generated at the decentralized level. In Costa Rica, for example, the National Biodiversity Institute (INBio) is involving local communities in drawing up a biodiversity inventory. And in cases where data collection takes place at a decentralized level, policy decisions based on geographical information need not be centralized either. The level at which policy decisions must be made should respond essentially to the scope of the externalities generated by such decisions. Decisions having to do with providing urban infrastructure or regulations on land use may be better made at the local level, provided the information exists and is known by the relevant decisionmakers. On the other hand, decisions involving broad geographical externalities—such as controlling water or air pollution or infectious diseases—naturally are better made at the regional, national, or even international levels.

Effective dissemination of information is essential not only for government policymakers, but also for those who may suffer the consequences of problems caused or influenced by geography, most of whom are poor. Administrative procedures for obtaining zoning permits are often deliberately made vague and obscure to enable corruption. They can then be used as a means to extort money from people who have invested in houses or businesses on inadequate sites.

People often build homes in high-risk areas because there is no information available to them on the risks involved, or because that information has been manipulated or concealed. Huge losses suffered by agricultural producers could often be avoided if the quality of forecasting in the region regarding the weather and other natural hazards was improved and information better disseminated. Having available information on the frequency and intensity of natural hazards could also facilitate development of insurance markets, which are still in an incipient stage in Latin America. Countries where producers and investors are covered for hurricane risks by insurance do not suffer the recessionary effects following the disaster that countries without such coverage suffer. The Dominican Republic received compensation following Hurricane Georges in 1998 that amounted to around 2 percent of GDP, a powerful stimulus for the construction industry and a factor in sustaining a high economic growth rate even in the aftermath of a disaster. Access to insurance and other financial services is particularly crucial for low-income households, the informal sector, and small businesses.

The problem of risk is obvious in the case of natural disasters, but there are others as well, such as agricultural risks and the risk of disease. Again, making information available can help. National governments can help people overcome the adverse effects of geography by disseminating information on production technologies for low-productivity or erosion-prone lands, methods of pest or disease control, and suitable techniques for building homes in geographically vulnerable areas.

Although it is essential that governments generate and disseminate such information, the marketplace remains the more effective dissemination mechanism if it operates correctly. Low land prices in areas that are disaster prone or outside the scope of urban public services often attract the poor, leading to construction of vulnerable settlements. The marketplace can be used to head off such developments. For example, a system of subsidies for those who build new houses may be more effective than an administrative or policing procedure in resettling the inhabitants of a high-risk area. The most effective way to contain erosion may be the use of a subsidy to encourage use of a new technology to displace inappropriate ones. To encourage a community to preserve a scarce resource (a nature reserve, for example), the best approach may be to promote a market for that resource (ecological tourism, for example) rather than preventing it from being used, which reduces its potential value.

To respond to market signals, people must have mobility. An area of low agricultural productivity with poor health conditions can become a poverty trap if policies discourage migration toward areas with better opportunities. Fear of migration from the countryside to the city, deeply rooted in the minds of Latin American leaders, has often translated into subsidies to unproductive farming sectors and rural areas. Further, surveys in the mid-1990s showed that nearly half of the small farmers in Honduras, Paraguay, and Colombia did not have land titles (López and Valdés 1996, cited by López 1996). This not only limits their mobility but also reduces access to credit and discourages investment (Carter and Olinto 1996; López 1996).[4] In disaster-prone areas, lack of land titling discourages owners from making investments that could lower risks and hinders any resettlement policy. In short, problems that limit mobility reinforce rather than alleviate the adverse effects of geography.

Urban Policies

There is ample empirical evidence that public investments in urban infrastructure have a positive effect on private productivity (Lobo and Rantisi 1999, p. 1; Seitz 1995). High-quality transportation infrastructure and integrated transportation systems (roads, rail, and ports) contribute to higher productivity in industrial production and greater exports by facilitating the movement of merchandise and goods. Efficient transportation systems also increase the mobility of urban residents and access to jobs and decrease average commuting time. As Latin American cities grow in size—the metropolitan area of Saõ Paulo now covers an astounding 8,000 square kilometers (World Resources Institute 1996, p. 59)—efficient transportation systems are all the more necessary.

Car ownership per capita is still relatively low in Latin America, which makes public transportation particularly important in increasing urban productivity. Public transportation is less costly in terms of energy use, air pollution, and congestion. While underground systems are effective, their cost is extremely high compared with other public transportation such as buses. Curitiba in Brazil is often cited as an example of a good public transportation system. By combining land use planning and reserved lanes for buses, Curitiba has managed to limit congestion and pollution. Most of the city's travelers use public transportation systems (Gilbert 1998, pp. 166–67).

The provision of urban services is also important to boost urban productivity (Peterson, Kingsley, and Telgrasky 1991, as cited by Devas and Rakodi 1993, p. 268). Although the percentage of urban dwellers with access to potable water, sewerage, waste disposal, and electricity has increased substantially over the last 30 years, equipment in many cities is still lagging and average satisfactory percentages hide great levels of inequalities between low- and high-income neighborhoods. Access to these basic services has an important impact on the health of urban residents and the incidence of communicable diseases. Reliable water and electricity supply is also an important precondition for the development of a diversified industrial base in the large metropolitan area. Geographical conditions and mismanagement threaten the future availability of water supply in several cities in the region, including Mexico City and Lima (Brennan 1994, pp. 244–45).

Adequate urban infrastructure is also essential to limit the adverse effects of natural disasters. As the total amount of urban assets increases with urban growth and economic development, the economic and financial risk associated with natural disasters is multiplied. In countries where the primary city is located in a hazard-prone area, the risk is even greater, since national economic activity is highly dependent on a small geographical area. Such were the effects of the 1999 earthquake in the main industrial region of Turkey.

To upgrade urban infrastructure, municipal management in Latin America has to improve. Better mobilization of local resources through taxation and usage fees and local public-private partnerships is essential to provide an adequate level of infrastructure and services in urban environments. Better management capacity at the municipality level is needed, as well as closer cooperation between municipalities that make up major metropolitan areas. Cities must adopt simplified, transparent, and enforceable procedures that better regulate urban growth but do not paralyze private initiative and push more activity into the informal sector. Innovative solutions have to be found to optimize the use of urban space while preventing the increase in land prices from eliminating low-income housing options.

Finally, public policy should also attempt to control and moderate urban concentration by supporting deconcentration and the emergence of new or multinuclear cities. While concentration is shown to be an advantage in the first phases of economic development, its positive effects decrease as income grows and cities become too large (Henderson 2000, pp. 1–3). In contrast, the presence of several urban centers in a country fosters healthy competition between cities to attract economic activity and investments. This competition leads to a better supply of infrastructure and urban services, as well as tax systems more favorable to business development (Seitz 1995, p. 138).

Spatial Organization

Decentralization is an important tool for taming and exploiting geography because of the wide variety of ways that human and physical geography can affect development, ranging from natural disasters to population trends. It is difficult to imagine a centralized decision-making system that could respond adequately to the variety of needs and restrictions imposed by geography on different locations, especially in countries as geographically heterogeneous as those in Latin America. Because identifying local preferences and needs is often easier for local and regional governments, a better match between demand for and supply of public services can be expected. For instance, decentralization tends to produce more investment in infrastructure and better quality infrastructure (Estache 1995).

However, a single decentralization model cannot be effective to solve the range of problems posed by physical and human geography. In Latin America, local governments—municipalities, provinces, or districts, according to the term used in each country—are organized basically in the same manner, without taking into account differences in size, location, or other basic geographical and socioeconomic conditions. In Brazil, for example, the same rules apply to São Paulo (population of 8.5 million) or Pirapora de Bom Jesus (population of 4,850) (Estache 1995, p. 10). The result in more prosperous locations is that the potential for better organization and service delivery goes untapped, especially in countries with more centralized government structures. Meanwhile, less geographically and economically fortunate localities can be overwhelmed by administrative demands and responsibilities.

Some countries have begun to break this straitjacket by using more flexible and adaptable decentralization processes. In Colombia and Venezuela, some responsibilities for providing road infrastructure and other public services are assigned by contract to subnational governments according to their administrative and technical capability. In Colombia, the process has also involved nongovernmental bodies such as the coffee producers' association or oil companies, which have assumed some responsibilities for providing infrastructure.

A single decentralization structure is ineffective from a geographical standpoint as well, since some of the most important effects of geography are not clearly localized, or because they generate externalities that are significant for other localities or regions. For example, illnesses or plagues affecting several localities cannot be eradicated by any locality alone. An appropriate technology for containing erosion in river basins and preventing mudslides or floods is unlikely to be developed by the locality causing the problem, partly for cost reasons, but particularly because other localities may be more affected by the danger than is the locality where the problem originates. Hence, the locality where the problem lies will expect other affected localities to help solve it. A highway built to end the geographical isolation of one region will have to cross many other areas to be useful, and obviously will not be undertaken by any one locality alone. Because of ever-changing human and economic geography, spatial organization must also be dynamic and adept at change. For instance, the geographical expansion of cities might cross regional borders and create serious jurisdictional and coordination issues, such as in the case of Mexico City.

Each of these examples suggests the need for a different level of geographical organization. The problem of a pest that affects a specific crop may require only the organization of producers, while a tropical disease may demand national or even global intervention. Mitigating the risk of natural disasters demands some degree of centralization for identification of national priorities, allocation of federal resources, and development of integrated response systems. But at the same time, it requires decentralized implementation of mitigation and preparedness efforts in cooperation with local communities. Addressing a problem of erosion may involve a group effort by municipalities that share a river basin. Construction of a highway may require cooperation both by the isolated areas to where the road is being built and by others that may benefit in some other way from the new investment.

Hence, the form of decentralization suitable for solving some problems may be very different from that needed to solve others. It is not just a matter of different levels of aggregation (municipal, state, national), but also of different types of groupings (groups of municipalities or zones that may or may not correspond to existing territorial units, or combinations of different levels of government).

Although in principle it might be possible to define the level and type of grouping of localities sharing the same geographical problem or benefit, this does not mean that cooperation will be easy or even feasible owing to different local preferences or conflicts of interest. Problems of coordinating more than a few municipalities may prove intractable and are not always necessarily solved by grouping the municipalities at an intermediate territorial level. In other words, geographical heterogeneity imposes demands for institutional development that may be difficult to meet, trapping the more geographically fragmented countries in situations of low economic and social development.[5] The excessive number of political jurisdictions exacerbates these problems in many Latin American countries. That is, the political fragmentation of territory hinders solving economic and social problems, particularly those that are geographical in origin. As we saw in chapter 2, Mexican states with a greater density of municipalities have significantly lower levels of development. Many Latin American countries have an excessive number of political jurisdictions, especially at the municipal level. Panama, with a population of 3 million, has 67 municipalities, whereas El Salvador, with a population only twice as large, has 262 municipalities. The number of municipalities in Venezuela rose from 200 in 1985 to 333 in 1998, and in Colombia there are now more than 1,000 municipalities.

Although political fragmentation usually has deep historical roots, laws that encourage the creation of new municipalities have reinforced the trend. For example, the setting of a fixed component of fiscal transfers per municipality (in addition to the variable component by population or by other variables) leads to the creation of small municipalities. Electoral rules that assign to each territorial unit a basic number of seats in legislative bodies have the same consequence.

All of these complications point up the fact that while decentralization is an essential instrument for taming geography, it is not a simple instrument. In principle, three conditions are needed for successful decentralization. First, the local decisionmaking process must be democratic, in the sense that the costs and benefits of decisions are transparent and all those affected have an equal opportunity to affect those decisions. Second, the costs of local decisions must be borne completely by those making them, and not transferred to other territorial units or to the central government. And third, the benefits must also be circumscribed to the participants. When these conditions are all met, the responsibilities and their financing can be totally transferred to subnational governments or organizations. Unfortunately, few if any of the problems posed by geography allow for these conditions to be fully met. This does not mean that decentralization must be rejected, but rather that it ought to be designed in each case in such a way that all participants have incentives similar to those that would exist if such conditions were indeed met.

Solving the problem of transparency requires systems of democratic participation in decisionmaking and public control of local government (as well as the generation and dissemination of information, as discussed in the previous section). Although municipal governments are now popularly elected in most Latin American countries, municipalities are not always the most suitable entity for decentralization. Decentralizing responsibilities to other organizations or governmental levels must be backed by similar democratic decisionmaking procedures. For example, in instances where coffee producer organizations have responded to a set of information externalities and problems that are largely of geographical origin, the most favorable results have occurred in countries where those organizations used democratic procedures (Bates 1997).

To prevent the costs of local decisions from being transferred to other entities or government levels, clear and credible budgetary restrictions must be imposed. That requires clearly defining the responsibilities to be assumed by the subnational government or the relevant decentralization entity. Similarly, if transfers are received from the national government for fulfilling these functions, such transfers must be determined by the level and quality of the services provided, not by the costs incurred or by an acquired right, as happens when transfers are a percentage of central government revenues. Finally, the lower-level government must also have very strict debt limits in keeping with its own revenue-generating ability.

Avoiding deficiencies or excesses in the provision of certain services that generate positive (or negative) externalities to other territorial units requires creation of a system for transfers (or taxes) from the central government to providers. Some countries have set up joint financing procedures for certain investments that generate significant geographical externalities, such as highway construction, wastewater treatment, or control of air pollution.

Latin American countries are abandoning the traditional centralism of their institutions and policies in favor of more decentralized and participatory systems. The success of that strategy will depend largely on its ability to incorporate new dimensions of human and physical geography into the design and implementation of new policies.

Notes

1. Ravallion (2000), as cited by de Janvry and Sadoulet (2000).
2. However, those high returns may be partly due to selection bias, as successful experiences are easier to identify and attract more attention.
3. Using a simple regression to predict average life expectancy in 1995 based on the natural logarithm of GDP per capita, Latin American countries have an average life expectancy four years longer than would be predicted by GDP alone. If one also controls for tropical location, life expectancy in the region is eight years higher than expected. See also Inter-American Development Bank (2000, chapter 1).
4. Nevertheless, where efficient credit markets do not exist, a massive land titling policy can have adverse effects on distribution.
5. See Inter-American Development Bank (2000, chapter 4) for a discussion of this point and its implications for governability.

Abbreviations and Acronyms

BCG	Bacillus Calmette-Guerin (tuberculosis)
CEDEPRENAC	Coordination Center for the Prevention of Natural Disasters
CENEPI	Center for the Control of Epidemics (Brazil)
CGIAR	Consultative Group on International Agricultural Research
DANE	Departamento Administrativo Nacional de Estadistica (Colombia)
DPT	Diphtheria, tetanus, pertussis
ECLAC	Economic Commission for Latin America and the Caribbean
ENE	National Employment Survey
EPZ	Export processing zones
ESRI	Environmental Systems Research Institute
FAO	Food and Agriculture Organization of the United Nations
FONCODES	Fondo Nacional de Compensacion Social (Peru)
GDP	Gross domestic product
IBGE	Instituto Brasileiro de Geografia (Brazil)
ICD	International Classification of Diseases
IDB	Inter-American Development Bank
IFRC	International Federation of the Red Cross
IMF	Internatonal Monetary Fund
IMR	Infant mortality rate
INBio	National Biodiversity Institute (Costa Rica)

INE	Instituto Nacional de Estadistica (Bolivia)
INEGI	Instituto Nacional de Estadística, Geografía e Informática (Mexico)
LSMS	Living Standards Measurement Survey
NAFTA	North Atlantic Free Trade Agreement
NBER	National Bureau of Economic Research
OAS	Organization of American States
OECD	Organisation for Economic Co-operation and Development
OFDA	Office of Foreign Disaster Assistance
PAHO	Pan American Health Organization
PRI	Partido Revolucionario Institucional (Mexico)
SIM	System of mortality information
UBN	Unsatisfied basic needs
UDAPE	Unidad de Análisis de Politica Económica
UNCTAD	United Nations Conference on Trade and Development
UNDP	United Nations Development Programme
UNEP	United Nations Environment Programme
UNFPA	United Nations Population Fund
UNICEF	United Nations Children's Fund
USAID	United States Agency for International Development
WEPZA	World Economic Processing Zones Association
WHO	World Health Organization

Bibliography

The word "processed" describes informally produced works that may not be commonly available through libraries.

Acemoglu, D., S. Johnson, and J. A. Robinson. 2001. "The Colonial Origins of Comparative Development: An Empirical Investigation." *American Economic Review* 91(5):1369–1401.

Ades, Alberto, and Edward L. Glaeser. 1995. "Trade and Circuses: Explaining Urban Giants." *Quarterly Journal of Economics* 110(1): 195–228.

Albala-Bertrand, J. M. 1993. *The Political Economy of Large Natural Disasters.* Oxford: Clarendon Press.

Alesina, Alberto, and Dani Rodrik. 1994. "Distributive Politics and Economic Growth." *Quarterly Journal of Economics* 109(2): 465–90.

Alves, Denisard, Robert Evenson, Elca Rosenberg, and Christopher Timmins. 2000. "Health, Climate and Development in Brazil: A Cross-Section Analysis." Research Network Working Paper No. 386. Inter-American Development Bank Research Department, Washington, D.C.

Arrieta, M. 1994. *Agricultura en Santa Cruz: de la encomienda colonial a la empresa modernizada (1559–1985).* La Paz: Instituto Latinoamericano de Investigaciones Sociales (ILDIS).

Azzoni, Carlos R., Naercio Menezes-Filho, Tatiane A. de Menezes, and Raul Silveira-Neto. 2000. "Geography and Income Convergence among Brazilian States." Latin American Research Network Working Paper No. 395. Inter-American Development Bank Research Department, Washington, D.C.

Barro, Robert J., and Xavier Sala-i-Martin. 1992. "Convergence." *Journal of Political Economy* 100(2): 223–51.

———. 1995. *Economic Growth*. New York: McGraw Hill.

Bates, Robert H. 1997. "Institutions and Development." In Diego Pizano and José Chalarca, *Coffee, Institutions and Economic Development*. Bogota: National Federation of Coffee Growers.

Bedi, Arjun S. 1999. "The Role of Information and Communication Technologies in Economic Development, A Partial Survey." Zentrum Fur Entwicklungsforschung (ZEF). Discussion Paper on Development Policy, Bonn University. May.

Bitrán, Ricardo, Cecilia Má, and Gloria Ubilla. 2000. "Geography, Health Status, and Health Investments: An Analysis of Peru." Latin American Research Network Working Paper No. 402. Inter-American Development Bank Research Department, Washington, D.C.

Bitrán, R., C. Riese, and L. Prieto. 1998. *Health Care Demand and Expenditure Study in Four Departments of Guatemala*. Guatemala City: National Institute of Guatemala, Ministry of Public Health and Social Welfare, and MACRO International.

Blum, Roberto, and Alberto Díaz Cayeros. 2002. "Rentier States and Geography in Mexico's Development." Latin American Research Network Working Paper No. 443. Inter-American Development Bank Research Department, Washington, D.C.

Brennan, Ellen. 1994. "Mega-City Management and Innovation Strategies: Regional Views." In Roland J. Fuchs et al., *Mega-City Growth and the Future*. New York: United Nations University Press.

Canning, David. 1998. "A Database of World Infrastructure Stocks 1950–1995." Harvard Institute for International Development. Available at http://www.cid.harvard.edu/Infra11.html. Processed.

Carter, Michael R., and Pedro Olinto. 1996. "Getting Institutions Right for Whom? The Wealth Differentiated Impact of Property Rights Reform on Investment and Income in Rural Paraguay." University of Wisconsin Department of Agricultural Economics. Processed.

Clarke, Caroline. 2000. "The Role of International Financing Institutions in Disaster Risk Management in Urban Areas: A Perspective from the Inter-American Development Bank." Paper presented at the Conference on After Disasters: The Impact of Natural Disaster on Urban Development and Public Health in Central America and the Caribbean, 10 January.

Coatesworth, John H. 1998. "Economic and Institutional Trajectories in Nineteenth-Century Latin America." In John H. Coatesworth and Alan M. Taylor (eds.), *Latin America and the World Economy Since 1800*. Cambridge, Mass.: Harvard University Press.

Coelho, Philip R. P., and Robert A. McGuire. 1997. "African and European Bound Labor in the British New World: The Biological Consequences of Economic Choices." *Journal of Economic History* 57(1): 83–115.

Coordination Center for the Prevention of Natural Disasters (CEDE-PRENAC). 1999. "Social and Ecological Vulnerability." Paper presented at the Stockholm Consultative Group Meeting on Central America's Reconstruction and Transformation. April.

CRED (Centre for Research on the Epidemiology of Disasters). 2000. "EM-DAT: The OFDA/CRED International Disaster Database 1900–1999." Université Catholique de Louvain. www.md.ucl.ac.-be/cred.

Crosby, Alfred W. 1972. *The Columbian Exchange: Biological and Cultural Consequences of 1492*. Westport, Conn.: Greenwood Press.

———. 1986. *Ecological Imperialism: The Biological Expansion of Europe, 900–1900*. Cambridge: Cambridge University Press.

Cuervo, L. M., and J. González. 1997. *Industria y ciudades en la era de la mundialización. Un enfoque socioespacial*. Bogota: CIDER-Colciencias-Tercer Mundo Editores.

Currie, Lauchlin Bernard. 1950. "The Basis of a Development Program for Colombia." Report of a mission headed by Lauchlin Currie and sponsored by the International Bank for Reconstruction and Development in collaboration with the Government of Colombia.

Curto de Casas, S. I., and R. U. Carcavallo. 1995. "Climate Change and Vector-borne Disease Distribution." *Social Science and Medicine* 40(11): 1437–40.

Deininger, Klaus, and Lyn Squire. 1996. "A New Data Set Measuring Income Inequality." *World Bank Economic Review* 10(3) September: 565–91.

de Janvry, Alain, and Elisabeth Sadoulet. 1998. "New Ways of Looking at Old Issues: Inequality and Growth." *Journal of Development Economics* 57(2): 259–87.

———. 2000. "Making Investment in the Rural Poor into Good Business: New Perspectives for Rural Development in Latin America." Paper presented at the Conference on Development of the Rural Economy and Poverty Reduction in LAC, at the Annual Meeting of the Inter-American Development Bank, New Orleans, March 25, 2000.

Departamento Administrativo Nacional de Estadística (DANE). 1997. Encuesta Nacional de Calidad de Vida, Colombia.

Devas, Nick, and Carole Rakodi (eds.). 1993. "Managing Fast Growing Cities." *Longman Scientific and Technical Journal* 268.

Diamond, Jared. 1997. *Guns, Germs, and Steel: The Fates of Human Societies.* New York: W. W. Norton.

Easterly, William, and Ross Levine. 1997. "Africa's Growth Tragedy: Policies and Ethnic Divisions." *Quarterly Journal of Economics* 112(4) November: 1203–50.

Echeverría, R. G. 1990. "Assessing the Impact of Agricultural Research." In R. Echeverría (ed.), *Methods for Diagnosing Research System Constraints and Assessing the Impact of Agricultural Research,* Vol. 2: *Assessing the Impact of Agricultural Research.* The Hague: ISNAR.

Economic Commission for Latin America and the Caribbean (ECLAC). 1999. "Honduras: evaluación de los daños ocasionados por el huracán Mitch, 1998: sus implicaciones para el desarrollo económico y social y el medio ambiente." ECLAC LC/MEX L.367.

———. 2000. "Confronting Natural Disasters: A Matter of Development." Paper presented at the Annual Meeting of the Inter-American Development Bank, 25–26 March, New Orleans, La.

Economist Intelligence Unit Country Report for Honduras, 1st Quarter 2000.

Engerman, Stanley L., and Kenneth L. Sokoloff. 1997. "Factor Endowments, Institutions, and Differential Paths of Growth among New World Economies: A View from Economic Historians of the United States." In Stephen Haber (ed.), *How Latin America Fell Behind: Essays on the Economic Histories of Brazil and Mexico, 1800–1914.* Stanford, Calif.: Stanford University Press.

Environmental Systems Research Institute (ESRI). 1996. *Arc Atlas: Our Earth.* Redlands, Calif.: ESRI.

Escobal, Javier, and Máximo Torero. 2000. "Does Geography Explain Differences in Economic Growth in Peru?" Latin American Research Network Working Paper No. 389. Inter-American Development Bank Research Department, Washington, D.C.

Esquivel, Gerardo. 1999. Convergencia Regional en México, 1940–1995. *El Trimestre Económico. Fondo de Cultura Económica* 264. October-December.

———. 2000. "Geografía y desarrollo económico en México." Latin American Research Network Working Paper No. 389. Inter-American Development Bank Research Department, Washington, D.C.

Estache, A. 1995. "Decentralizing Infrastructure: Advantages and Limitations." World Bank Discussion Paper 290. Washington, D.C.

Evenson, Robert E., Carl E. Pray, and Mark W. Rosegrant. 1999. *Agricultural Research and Productivity Growth in India.* IFPRI Research Report No. 109.

Fagan, Brian. 1999. *Floods, Famines, and Emperors: El Niño and the Fate of Civilizations.* New York: Basic Books.

Fallon, Peter. 1998. "¿Es Possible que las Regiones Atrasadas de un País Alcancen a las Más Avanzadas?" World Bank Notas PREM 6 (July).

Fernández, C. 1999. *Agglomeration and Trade: The Colombian Case.* Bogota: Banco de la República.

Food and Agriculture Organization of the United Nations (FAO). 1999. The FAOSTAT Database. http://apps.fao.org/default.htm.

Forbes, Kristin. 1998. "Growth, Inequality, Trade, and Stock Market Contagion: Three Empirical Tests of International Economic Relationships." Ph.D. diss. Massachusetts Institute of Technology, Cambridge, Mass.

Fujita, Masahisa, Paul Krugman, and Anthony J. Venables. 1999. *The Spatial Economy: Cities, Regions, and International Trade.* Cambridge, Mass.: MIT Press.

Gallup, John Luke, Steven Radelet, and Andrew Warner. 1998. "Economic Growth and the Income of the Poor." Harvard Institute for International Development. Processed.

Gallup, John Luke, and Jeffrey D. Sachs. 1998. "The Economic Burden of Malaria." Harvard Institute for International Development. Available at http://www.hiid.harvard.edu/research/newnote.html# geogrowth.

———. 1999. "Agricultural Productivity and the Tropics." Center for International Development. Processed.

Gallup, John Luke, Jeffrey D. Sachs, and Andrew D. Mellinger. 1999. "Geography and Economic Development." In Boris Pleskovic and Joseph E. Stiglitz (eds.), *World Bank Annual Conference on Development Economics 1998.* Washington, D.C.: World Bank.

Galton, Francis. 1889. *Natural Inheritance.* London: Macmillan and Co.

Gaviria, Alejandro, and Carmen Pagés. 2002. "Patterns of Crime Victimization in Latin American Cities." *Journal of Development Economics* 67: 181–203.

Gaviria, Alejandro, and Ernesto Stein. 1999. "Urban Concentration in Latin America and the World." Inter-American Development Bank, Washington, D.C. Processed.

Gilbert, Alan. 1998. *The Latin American City*. Nottingham: Russell Press.

Glaeser, Edward L. 1998. "Are Cities Dying?" *Journal of Economic Perspectives* 12 (Spring): 139–60.

Glaeser, Edward L., and Bruce Sacerdote. 1996. "Why Is There More Crime in Cities?" National Bureau of Economic Research Working Paper 5430, Cambridge, Mass.

Gleick, James. 1999. *Faster: The Acceleration of Just about Everything*. New York: Pantheon Books.

Gouesset, V. 1998. *Bogotá: el nacimiento de una metrópoli*. Bogota: Tercer Mundo.

Hamer, Andrew Marsh. 1994. "Economic Impacts of Third World Megacities: Is Size the Issue?" In Roland J. Fuchs, Ellen Brennan, Joseph Chamie, Fu-Chen Lo, and Juha L. Uitto, *Mega-City Growth and the Future*. United Nations University Press.

Hamilton, J. 1970. "Del Magdalena a Bogotá." In *Viajeros extranjeros en Colombia, siglo XXI*. Cali: Carvajal.

Hardoy, Jorge E. 1989. *The Poor Die Young: Housing and Health in the Third World*. London: Earthscan.

Harris, M. 1987. *The Sacred Cow and the Abominable Pig: Riddles of Food and Culture*. New York: Simon and Schuster.

Heinl Jr., Robert Debs, and Nancy Gordon Heinl. 1978. *Written in Blood: The Story of the Haitian People 1492–1971*. Boston: Houghton Mifflin.

Henderson, Vernon. 2000. "The Effects of Urban Concentration on Economic Growth." National Bureau of Economic Research Working Paper 7503, Cambridge, Mass.

Huntington, Ellsworth. 1927. *Civilization and Climate*, 3rd ed. New Haven: Yale University Press.

Instituto Nacional de Estadística (INE). 1997a. *Migraciones de la población economicamente activa*. La Paz: Ministerio de Hacienda.

———. 1997b. *Salud en cifras: 1990–1995*. La Paz: Ministerio de Hacienda.

Inter-American Development Bank (IDB). 2000. *Social Protection for Equity and Growth*. Washington, D.C.: IDB.

International Federation of the Red Cross (IFRC). 1993. *World Disasters Report*. Dordrecht: Martinus Nijhoff.

———. 1997. *World Disasters Report*. Dordrecht: Martinus Nijhoff.

————. 1999. *World Disasters Report*. Dordrecht: Martinus Nijhoff.

International Monetary Fund (IMF). 2000. "Country Report for Honduras no. 00/5, January." Washington, D.C.

Keller, Wolfgang. 2000. "Geographical Localization of International Technology Diffusion." National Bureau of Economic Research Working Paper 7509, Cambridge, Mass.

Landes, David. 1998. *The Wealth and Poverty of Nations*. New York: Norton.

La Porta, R., F. López de Silanes, A. Shleifer, and R. Vishny. 1998. "The Quality of Government." National Bureau of Economic Research Working Paper 6727, Cambridge, Mass.

Li, Hongyi, Lyn Squire, and Heng-fu Zou. 1998. "Explaining International and Intertemporal Variations in Income Inequality." *Economic Journal* 108(446): 26–43.

Living Standards Measurement Surveys (LSMS). 1985–6, 1994, 1997. Cuanto Institute, Lima.

Lobo, José, and Norma M. Rantisi. 1999. "Investments in Infrastructure as a Determinant of Metropolitan Productivity." *Growth and Change* 30 (Winter): 106–27.

López, Ramón. 1996. "Land Titles and Farm Productivity in Honduras." University of Maryland Department of Agriculture and Resource Economics. Processed.

López, Ramón, and Alberto Valdés. 1996. *Rural Poverty in Latin America*. Washington, D.C.: World Bank.

Maddison, Angus. 1995. *Monitoring the World Economy: 1820–1992*. Paris: Organisation for Economic Co-operation and Development.

Martens, W. J. M. 1998. "Climate Change, Thermal Stress and Mortality Changes." *Social Science & Medicine* 46(3): 331–44.

McCullough, David. 1977. *The Path between the Seas: The Creation of the Panama Canal, 1970–1914*. New York: Simon and Schuster.

McMichael, A. J., and A. Haines. 1997. "Global Climate Change: The Potential Effects on Health." *Review of Economics and Statistics* 62(2): 318–21.

McNeill, William H. 1976. *Plagues and Peoples*. Garden City, N.Y.: Anchor Press.

Meller, Patricio. 1995. "Chilean Export Growth, 1970–1990: An Assessment." In G. K. Helleiner (ed.), *Manufacturing for Export in the Developing World*. London and New York: Routledge.

———. 1996. "La maldición de los recursos naturales." *Archivos del Presente* 2(6) October. Buenos Aires.

Morales, Rolando, Erwin Galoppo, Luis Carlos Jemio, María Carmen Choque, and Natacha Morales. 2000. "Bolivia: Geografía y desarrollo económico." Latin American Research Network Working Paper No. 387. Inter-American Development Bank Research Department, Washington, D.C.

Münchener Rück VersicherungsGesellschaft. 2000. *Topics 2000, Natural Catastrophes: The Current Position.*

Munich Reinsurance Group. 1999. Press Release, March 15, 1999.

Office of Foreign Disaster Assistance (OFDA). 1999. *Significant Data on Major Disasters Worldwide, 1900–1995.* U.S. Agency for International Development, Washington, D.C.

Palerm, Angel. 1952. *The Tajin Totonac.* Washington, D.C.: Smithsonian Institution, Institute of Social Anthropology.

Pampana, E. J., and P. F. Russell. 1955. *Malaria: A World Problem.* Geneva: World Health Organization.

Pan American Health Organization (PAHO). 1998. *Health in the Americas,* Vol. 1. Washington, D.C.: PAHO.

Pan American Health Organization and World Health Organization (PAHO/WHO). 1994. *A World Safe from Natural Disasters.* Washington, D.C.: PAHO/WHO.

Parsons, J. 1997. *La colonización antioqueña en el occidente colombiano.* Bogota: Banco de la República/El Áncora Editores.

Peña Herrera, C. 1986. "El desarrollo de la geografía en el Perú." In Ernesto Yepes (ed.), *Estudios de historia de la ciencia en el Perú.* Lima: Sociedad Peruana de Historia de la Ciencia y la Tecnología.

Persson, Torsten, and Guido Tabellini. 1994. "Is Inequality Harmful for Growth?" *American Economic Review* 84(3): 600–21.

Peterson, G. E., G. T. Kingsley, and J. P. Telgrasky. 1991. *Urban Economics and National Development.* Washington, D.C.: U.S. Agency for International Development.

Posada, E. 1998. *El Caribe colombiano: una historia regional.* Bogota: Banco de la República/El Áncora Editores.

Pritchett, Lant, and Lawrence H. Summers. 1996. "Wealthier Is Healthier." *Journal of Human Resources* 31(4): 841–68.

Pulgar Vidal, J. 1946. *Geografía del Perú: las ocho regiones naturales,* 10th ed. Lima: Editorial Peisa.

Radelet, Steven C., and Jeffrey D. Sachs. 1998. "Shipping Costs, Manufactured Exports, and Economic Growth." Harvard Institute for International Development. Available at http://www.hiid.harvard.edu/pub/other/geodev.html.

Ravallion, M. 2000. *On the Urbanization of Poverty*. Washington, D.C.: World Bank, Development Economics Research Group.

Ravallion, M., and Q. Wodon. 1997. "Poor Areas, or Only Poor People?" World Bank Policy Research Working Paper 1798. World Bank, Washington, D.C.

Richardson, Harry W., and Peter M. Townroe. 1986. "Regional Policies in Developing Countries." In Peter Nijkamp (ed.), *Handbook of Regional and Urban Economics*. Vol. 1. Amsterdam: North Holland.

Ridley, Matt. 1999. *Genome. The Autobiography of a Species in 23 Chapters*. New York: Harper Collins.

Sachs, Jeffrey. 1999. "Helping the World's Poorest." *The Economist* 352(8132). August 14.

———. 2000. "Notes on a New Sociology of Economic Developments." In Lawrence E. Harrison and Samuel P. Huntington (eds.), *Culture Matters. How Values Shape Human Progress*. New York: Basic Books.

Sánchez, Fabio, and Jairo Núñez. 2000. "Geography and Economic Development in Colombia: A Municipal Approach." Latin American Research Network Working Paper No. 408. Inter-American Development Bank Research Department, Washington, D.C.

Seitz, Helmut. 1995. "The Productivity and Supply of Urban Infrastructure." *Annals of Regional Sciences* 29:121–41. Springer Verlag.

Strahler, Alan H., and Arthur N. Strahler. 1992. *Modern Physical Geography*, 4th ed. New York: John Wiley and Sons.

Tanzi, Vito, and Hamid Davoodi. 1997. "Corruption, Public Investment and Growth." IMF Working Paper No. 97/139. International Monetary Fund, Washington, D.C.

Thompson, E. T. 1941. "The Climatic Theory of the Plantation." *Agricultural History* 60 (January).

Tobler, W., U. Deichmann, J. Gottsegen, and K. Maloy. 1995. "The Global Demography Project." National Center for Geographic Information and Analysis Technical Report TR-95-6, April.

Unidad de Análisis de Política Económica (UDAPE). 1998. *Dossier de Estadísticas Económicas.* La Paz: Ministerio de Hacienda.

United Nations Development Programme (UNDP). 1996. *Urban Agglomerations, 1950–2015.* UNDP Population Division.

United Nations Environment Programme (UNEP). 2000. *Global Environment Outlook 2000.* New York: Oxford University Press.

United Nations Population Fund (UNFPA). 1999. *The State of World Population 1999.* Available at http://www.unfpa.org/swp/swp-main.htm.

Urquiola, Miguel, Lykke Andersen, Eduardo Antelo, José Luis Evia, and Osvaldo Nina. 1999. "Geography and Development in Bolivia: Migration, Urban and Industrial Concentration, Welfare, and Convergence: 1950–1992." Latin American Research Network Working Paper No. 385. Inter-American Development Bank Research Department, Washington, D.C.

Weiner, Jonathan. 1999. *Time, Love and Memory. A Great Biologist and His Quest for the Origins of Behavior.* New York: Vintage Books.

Welcome Trust. 1999. *An Audit of International Activity in Malaria Research.* London: The Welcome Trust.

Williams, E. 1964. *Capitalism and Slavery.* London: Andre Deutch Limited.

Wittofogel, K. 1981. *Oriental Despotism: A Comparative Study of Total Power.* New York: Vintage Books.

World Bank. 1994. *World Development Report. Infrastructure.* Washington, D.C.: World Bank.

———. 1997. *World Development Report. The State in a Changing World.* Washington, D.C.: World Bank.

———. 1998. *World Development Indicators 1998.* CD-ROM. World Bank, Washington, D.C.

———. 1999a. "Brazil, Rio de Janeiro: A City Study." Report 19747-BR. Vol. II. Washington, D.C.

———. 1999b. *Managing Disaster Risks in Mexico.* Washington, D.C.: World Bank.

World Economic Processing Zones Association (WEPZA). 1997. *WEPZA International Directory of Export Processing Zones and Free Trade Zones,* 3rd ed. Flagstaff, Ariz.: The Flagstaff Institute.

World Health Organization (WHO). 1967. "Malaria Eradication in 1966." *WHO Chronicle* 21(9):373–88.

————. 1990. *Tropical Diseases*. TDR-CTD/HH90.1. Geneva: WHO.

————. 1997. "World Malaria Situation in 1994, Part I." *WHO Weekly Epidemiological Record* 36:269–74.

World Resources Institute. 1996. *World Resources 1996–1997*. New York: Oxford University Press.

Index